# ARCHITECTS' HOUSES

"A good house is a created
thing made of many parts
economically. It speaks not
just of the materials from
which it is made, but of the
intangible rhythms, spirits,
and dreams of people's lives.
Its site is only a tiny piece
of the real world, yet this
place is made to seem like
an entire world. In its parts
it accommodates important
human activities, yet in
sum it expresses an attitude
toward life."

Charles Moore

# ARCHITECTS' HOUSES

## MICHAEL WEBB

Princeton Architectural Press, New York

# ARCHITECTS' HOUSES

# INTRODUCTION

All talented architects deserve the opportunity to live in houses they've designed for themselves. They've earned that right by thinking long and hard about the art of shaping space, channeling light, and finding inventive ways to construct shelter. Such endeavors should have given them a heightened appreciation of materials, the craft of building, and the need to respond to context, whether urban or rural. All the architects featured in this book share a keen appreciation of nature and the urgent need to reduce their carbon footprint. They have drawn upon a rich history of residential architecture, and use their own houses as laboratories in which to test new ideas, products, and technologies. Architects' houses can be a statement of principles and a practical demonstration of their talents. They can also be radical manifestos or prototypes for multiple housing.

Most people settle, from necessity or choice, for a house as standardized as the cars we drive or the clothes we wear. Few have any architectural quality; they are merely the profitable product of builders and developers. The rich can command more space and opulence but rarely achieve anything of true distinction; for the rest of humanity, a single-family house of any size is becoming an unattainable luxury if one chooses to live in a big city. That gives architects the chance—the obligation, even—to set an example by creating new models: houses that are affordable, sustainable, and tailored to individual needs, rather than the mass market. They have the freedom to please themselves and create anything that their budget, local regulations, and Nimby-ish neighbors will allow. But the temptation to take risks is tempered by the realization that they will have to live in their creations and accept full responsibility for any shortcomings.

Remarkably few make the attempt. Cost has become the greatest deterrent: no matter how economical the construction, the price of land continues to soar, and undeveloped plots are scarce in urban areas. Many architects, like the shoemaker whose children went barefoot, are too busy with their practices to design their own dwellings. It's much easier to lease an apartment that's conveniently close to the office, and which requires no maintenance.

Le Corbusier spent the early years of his practice experimenting on clients and writing polemics, but then made his home in the penthouse of a restrained apartment block he'd designed on the outskirts of Paris. Berthold Lubetkin let his imagination soar in designing a habitat for the penguins at London Zoo, but took a more considered approach when creating an apartment for himself on the upper floor of his Highpoint tower in London. Contemporary practitioners follow the lead of those pioneers, although they seldom get the chance to design an entire apartment building with a penthouse for themselves— as Norman Foster did on the south bank of the Thames.

Some architects prefer living in a period house or loft as a contrast to the work they do every day or as a found object to hollow out and remodel. Richard Meier, the maestro of purist white houses, spends his summers and weekends in a century-old East Hampton farmhouse, as a retreat from his Manhattan apartment. Richard Rogers paid homage to the Maison de Verre in Paris within a pair of Georgian terrace houses in the Chelsea district of London.

For this book, I've selected thirty houses that architects have built for themselves around the world over the past decade, focusing on the creative process. At the midway point is a survey of earlier models, from Thomas Jefferson's Monticello to more recent achievements. They differ widely, in size, material, character, and location. There are urban infills, rustic retreats, experiments, and fusions of new and old. They all make a statement, whether modest or ambitious, and each reflects the personality and tastes of its owner. Although they are all unique, there are common themes too. Inspiration comes from art, nature, or other architects. There's an emphasis on the elemental: transparency, mass, and void; raw surfaces enlivened by the play of light and shade. There's a free flow of space within, and an openness to outdoors, even in cold, wet locations. Framed views of nature complement artworks and furniture the owners have created or collected.

All have been built from the ground up, except for a radical remodel in the south of France and a house in Spain, where new live–work spaces complement a medieval complex. The featured architects have accepted the challenge of doing something out of the ordinary, turning constraints to advantage. They provide different answers to a crucial question: how can a house enrich lives and its surroundings?

Spacious or frugal, refined or rough-edged, daring or reductive, these adventurous dwellings should inspire other architects and everyone who would like to design or commission a house that is one of a kind.

# NORMAN FOSTER

# LA VOILE

# CAP FERRAT, FRANCE

The best architects welcome constraints, as a challenge to their creativity and problem-solving skills. Lord Foster's career is full of such encounters, including the Sackler Galleries at the Royal Academy in London, where an uncompromisingly new wing is juxtaposed with the eighteenth-century original, and the Médiathèque in Nîmes, where a steel and glass pavilion engages a Roman temple in a graceful *pas de deux*. The house that Foster and some colleagues built for his family on Cap Ferrat was much smaller than both these projects, but no less exacting.

Foster and his wife, Elena, liked this particular stretch of coast, for its natural beauty and convenient access to the airport at Nice. The problem was that the French government, confronted with the venality of local mayors who have conspired in the degradation of the Côte d'Azur, decided to administer planning controls from Paris, enforce them strictly, and protect this peninsula from unsightly

development. "You couldn't demolish or build anything; all you could do was convert," says Foster. "A pretty elastic word, although the rules were quite complex. The only property we could find was a five-story tower—a depressing looking building from the 1950s. It was the most extreme exercise in ingenuity to create what we did. Any sane person looking at the house would have said, 'You are absolutely mad!'"

Foster sketched his options for transforming this stack of floors and cell-like rooms into a light-filled belvedere that would draw in the natural beauty of the Mediterranean landscape, and provide a haven for family and friends. The unsightly stump was pushed out towards the street and, at the base, with a podium of four guest rooms, whose roof forms a terrace for a four-story living/dining room that acts as the social heart of the house. "The building and demolition work was like keyhole surgery," explains Juan Vieira,

Two curved steel beams and a skein of steel cables support a canopy of stretched canvas that shades the pool. A terrace for the four-story living/dining room extends over a podium of four guest rooms.

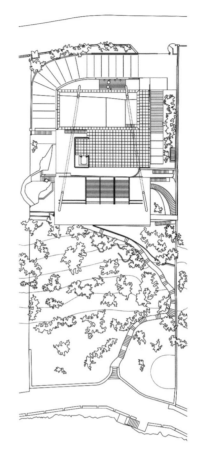

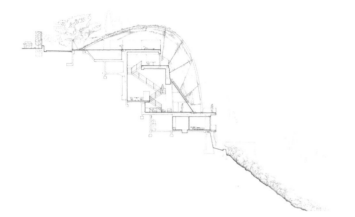

Seven levels were accommodated within the volume of the original structure, which could not be extended. Translucent glass sliders conceal the upper level and pool terrace from the street (opposite).

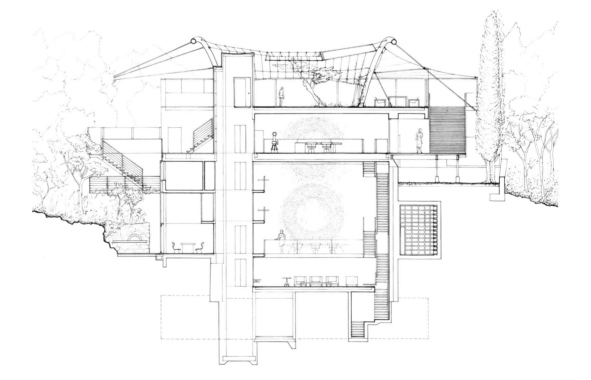

a member of the design team. "We would demolish then rebuild, bit by bit, and carve the openings out while keeping the line of the wall. Because of the slope of the site, a tall crane was used to drop a miniature digger into the house, and this was used to excavate the interior and the earth to create the bedrooms."

The house has seven levels, and it was hard to shoehorn them into the original envelope. The tolerances were down to millimeters. "Everyone in the area infringes the code, but we had an argument over the crane with the local hotel," Foster recalls. "The manager revenged himself by alerting the authorities. A pack of gendarmes and surveyors descended on the site and spent the whole day with tape measures trying to fault us. They were furious to discover that everything had been done by the book."

To open the living/dining room to the terrace, Foster designed a facade of two framed glass panels weighing 18 tonnes, which slide apart like stage curtains. That allowed cooling breezes to flow through the house, but the opening required a sun shade, one that would give the house a new signature. Foster has a passion for flying—he once cited a Boeing 747 as his favorite structure—and his architecture has always had a tensile elegance founded on an economy of means, even when it has to be massively reinforced. (Early in his career, Buckminster Fuller asked him, "How much does your building weigh, Mr Foster?")

In Cap Ferrat, inspiration came not from the air but from a billowing sail skimming across the Mediterranean. Two curved steel beams and a skein of steel cables support a canopy of stretched canvas that

shades the pool. Vines soften the cables in summer, providing additional protection, and drop their leaves in winter to allow the sun to warm the interior.

The house has the quality of a theater, in which tiers of seating look out onto nature's stage. To animate the rear wall of the living/dining room, Foster brought in Richard Long, a favorite artist of his, to create a site-specific mural out of mud from the site, much as Long had done on a larger scale in the atrium of the Hearst Tower in New York, where Foster + Partners had transformed Joseph Urban's unfinished office building. La Voile, however, is more than a spectacle: a three-story service core to the south includes a kitchen, laundry, and staff rooms, with a lift to link the different levels. Passive strategies allow the house to be warmed and cooled with a minimal reliance on mechanical equipment.

Sadly, Foster was unable to acquire the neighboring site for an extension, and, needing more room for a growing family, sold the property to the CEO of Finnish design house Marimekko, who had fallen in love with the house and its furnishings.

"It was the most extreme exercise in ingenuity to create what we did. Any sane person looking at the house would have said, 'You are absolutely mad!'"

Norman Foster

# BUZZ YUDELL & TINA BEEBE

# TREE HOUSE

# SANTA MONICA, CALIFORNIA

From the street, this house appears as a linear sequence of monopitch redwood barns, a neighborly response to traditional bungalows at the bottom of a canyon. It is aligned north–south, with rooms and courtyards opening off a linear gallery and looking out to the trees on either side. The exterior is impassive; the interior feels transparent and infused with natural light.

This is the fourth ground-up house that this long-married couple have built for themselves, and it incorporates elements they enjoyed in its predecessors: an Italianate residence in Malibu, an oceanfront compound at Sea Ranch, and a lofty cube in Santa Monica. The first two contained memories of Charles Moore, Yudell's mentor and former partner; he and Beebe decided to sell the third before

it was overwhelmed by mega-mansions. That's unlikely to happen in Rustic Canyon, where the bohemians and artists who first settled this bucolic enclave of LA have been succeeded by professionals and creatives who are determined to maintain its traditional character, while accepting modestly scaled modernism.

"I had people in the office working on the design, and then woke up one Saturday, sketched a new scheme over the weekend, and made my own model on Monday morning," recalls Yudell. "It's a simple, syncopated diagram, based on a 3×6m grid, and the eccentric corner angles are taken from the plan of the site. The complexity comes from the way you move through it, and the diagonal views complement the carefully proportioned

Each of the principal rooms has three or even four exposures to views, as well as to a garden of native, drought-resistant plantings. All of them open onto courtyards that serve as outdoor living spaces.

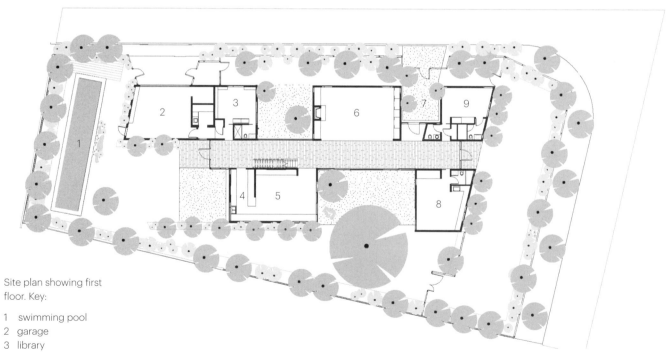

Site plan showing first
floor. Key:

1   swimming pool
2   garage
3   library
4   kitchen
5   living room
6   living/dining room
7   entry court
8   studio
9   guest room

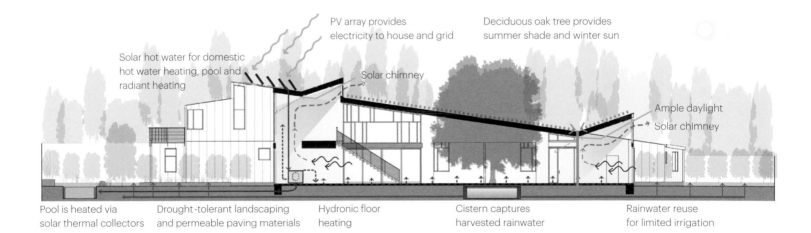

Solar hot water for domestic
hot water heating, pool and
radiant heating

PV array provides
electricity to house and grid

Deciduous oak tree provides
summer shade and winter sun

Solar chimney

Ample daylight

Solar chimney

Pool is heated via
solar thermal collectors

Drought-tolerant landscaping
and permeable paving materials

Hydronic floor
heating

Cistern captures
harvested rainwater

Rainwater reuse
for limited irrigation

rectangular rooms while imparting a sense of movement. Alvar Aalto's Maison Louis Carré outside Paris was a source of inspiration."

The gallery tilts up from the entry to a staircase at the north end. This ascends to both the master suite and Yudell's corner study, which feels like a tree house. Beebe preferred to have a ground-floor painting studio beside the entry, but set apart from the rest of the house. Each of the principal rooms has three or even four exposures to views, as well as to a garden of native, drought-resistant plantings, and all of them open onto courtyards that serve as outdoor living spaces. A huge, century-old English oak was nursed back to health and now provides summer shade while allowing sun to penetrate the house in winter. The ocean is only a mile away so the climate is temperate year-round, but the owners are aiming for net-zero energy

consumption, employing photovoltaic and solar panels for heating water, as well as a variety of passive strategies. There's also a cistern to collect rainwater.

"This is a big house but we use every part of it," says Beebe, who was involved in all aspects of the design and drew on her expertise in color, honed during the years she worked with Ray Eames. The vibrant and subtle tones that Beebe has employed here recall those that animated the earlier houses. "This is a woodsy site and we wanted the house to be warmed by organic colors," she explains. "Terracotta evokes a Roman villa—we've traveled in Italy a lot. I used coffee grounds in the plaster for the chimney at Sea Ranch and it smelled wonderful for a year. I tried a sample here with a different brand of coffee and it came out white, so I tried tea leaves but the effect was spotty, like a leopard. Another version emerged hairy from the leaves. Finally, I tried several tints and a little bit of tea. We did the chimney three times—each batch came out differently. You have to wait a week for it to dry before you know what you've got."

Beebe's experimentation tested the patience of the contractor, but the final result justified her efforts. A wall in the powder room was tinted salmon, the guest bedroom has an expanse of blue, and Yudell requested green for his study. The other walls required no special attention, for the steel-troweled Venetian plaster had just the right off-white tone. The couple searched long and far to secure honey-toned French limestone pavers, and complemented them with French oak

cabinetry. Tiny suspended light globes like jellyfish hover within the gallery. An open staircase of cantilevered, steel-lined oak treads ascends to the study, with its attic-like ceiling and tree-shaded deck. Oak cabinets enclose a dressing room beside the master bedroom.

Furnishings include two steel console tables from a now-defunct art gallery, as well as a chaise of composite ribs that Yudell designed for an exhibition sponsored by Formica and auctioned by the Rosenthal Contemporary Art Center in Cincinnati. There's an eclectic mix of paintings and prints, plus shelves of books that are there to be read, not stacked as ornaments on coffee tables.

An axial gallery tilts up from the entry to a staircase at the north end (below). This ascends to the master suite (opposite).

# SMILJAN RADIĆ

# HOUSE FOR THE POEM OF THE RIGHT ANGLE

# VILCHES, CHILE

Concrete is a much-favored material among Chilean architects, whose best work tends to be massive and restrained. Smiljan Radić stands outside the mainstream, not only for the expressiveness of his architecture, but also for his fondness for incorporating such natural elements as boulders into his structures. Inspired by one of the lithographs that Le Corbusier created to illustrate his *Poem of the Right Angle* (1947–53), Radić designed a vacation house of the same name in Vilches, a three-and-a-half-hour drive south of his home in Santiago. It's located on the property of his wife's family in the foothills of the Andes, close to the Altos de Lircay nature reserve. The gently sloping site is planted with young oaks, only one of which had to be felled to make room for the 165 sq m house, and several are enclosed within its central courtyard.

"We wanted a refuge more than a house," Radić explains, "a place for contemplation rather than viewing the landscape. It's something you feel, along with the sounds of birdsong and a nearby river. We know what is all around so we don't need to see it." The influence of Le Corbusier—the godfather of Latin American modernism—is evident in the three tapered skylights, which are derived from the "light cannons" that the master used to illuminate the chapel of La Tourette and the church at Firminy. For Radić, however, the lithograph was even more significant. "I loved that image for the link between shelter and a human body," he says. "The ambience was powerful for me and I hung it beside my desk. An elemental shelter is roofed by the hand of a man lying on his back. The floor is his body and in the background a nude woman contemplates a landscape traversed by a cloud, which relieves the darkness of the interior."

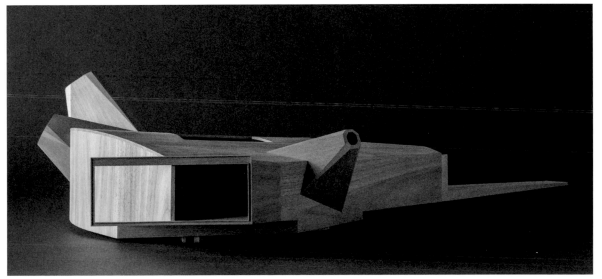

Radić created a 1/50th-scale wood model to explain the sculptural form to local workers, who had no prior experience of concrete construction.

Radić, who has a strong artistic impulse of his own, developed his ideas in a succession of sketches, which were later bought by the Department of Architecture at the Museum of Modern Art in New York. Like the sketches of Frank Gehry, they are free-form abstractions that only gradually coalesced into a buildable blueprint.

Because the site is remote and inaccessible to heavy equipment, the design had to be handcrafted by local workers who had no experience of concrete construction. Radić created a 1/50th-scale wood model to explain the sculptural form and spent several weeks on-site at the start of the project, to instruct the crew. The geometry is simpler than it appears, he says,

and the workers were able to erect a framework to support the forms, taking fifteen months to complete the job. The roughly shuttered concrete of the Unité d'Habitation in Marseilles was the product of necessity—a way of accommodating imprecise workmanship—before it became Le Corbusier's signature material. Here, the rough board marks give the house an organic character, as though it had grown out of the land.

Radić likens the form to a boat, with a bowed hull and the skylights as funnels. He considered adding a pigment to the mix, but the ultraviolet rays are so strong in Chile that the color would have faded swiftly. He painted the shell white, but

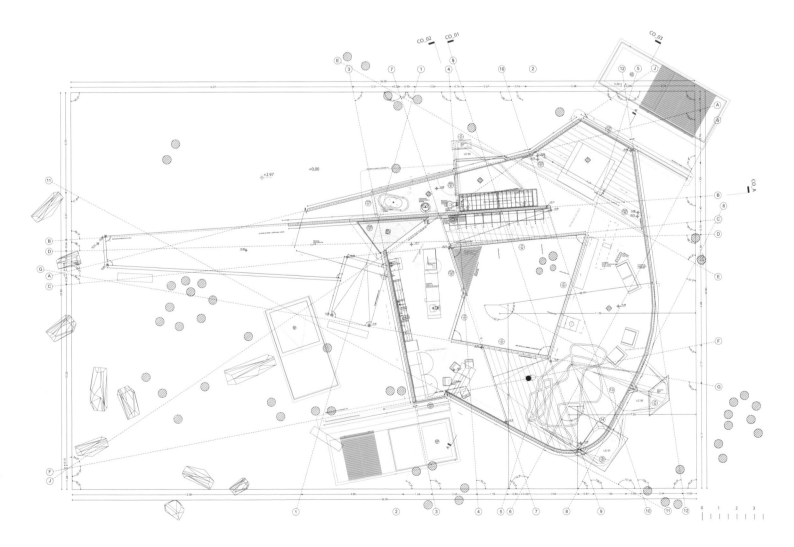

decided the effect was too assertive
and so switched to black, which merges
into the landscape. The house changes
character with the seasons, especially in
autumn, when the foliage turns golden
and mists blur the sharp outlines, or when
it is wreathed in snow. To extend it into the
forest and link it to other small structures
on the property, Radić employed his
trademark boulders, creating a stone garden
of 300 rocks from a neighboring quarry.

A ramp of polished black concrete leads
up to the entrance, and to the simply
furnished rooms that are ranged around
the glass-walled courtyard. Outer walls
arelined with Bolivian cedar, which was
selected for its wonderful aroma. Windows

open onto the courtyard for cross-
ventilation, and Radić and his wife, Chilean
artist Marcela Correa, have placed their bed
in a bay with a window wall that they leave
open on summer nights. The skylights rise
to a height of 7m, pulling in views of foliage
and sky, as well as patches of sunlight that
move slowly across the floor.

An espino wood sculpture by Correa
is suspended below the skylights,
and suggests writhing branches that have
strayed in from the forest. For Radić,
it evokes a body, as though another person
were sharing the house with the couple
when they go there for long weekends, in
search of seclusion or for family gatherings.

# RICHARD MURPHY

# HART STREET HOUSE

# EDINBURGH

A tightly compressed house on a confined lot responds to its historic neighbors and abounds in ideas and references. There are nine shifts of level, and a visiting architect likened it to a Rubik's Cube.

In Edinburgh, the New Town comprises stately terraces and squares dating back to the 1760s, and there's a deep suspicion of modernist interventions. Richard Murphy had long wanted to build a residence for himself, having remodeled a modest terrace house in his twenties. A project in the Old Town of Edinburgh failed to materialize, so he rented a mews house he had designed for an American client, and then another across the street. The only empty site he could find was half of an existing garden squeezed between two 1820s terraces. The buildable footprint was a tight 11×6 m, and the roof had to be steeply sloped on one side to preserve the right to light of a basement flat next door.

As an erudite architect who had designed twenty-five houses in Scotland, along with larger buildings, Murphy knew how hard it would be to win acceptance for a project that incorporated a lifetime of ideas and influences. Undeterred, he sketched

a three-bedroom house that would use smooth and indented ashlar to pick up on the adjacent terrace, and then cut into the masonry with new materials as though it were a ruin. "We've done the same with historic buildings; here, the conceit is that the stone is old," Murphy explains. "I have a language: expressed steel, glass block for light and privacy, burned timber and lead—and those materials form overlapping planes.

"And then," he continues, "we had a bit of fun. The New Town is all about facades; turn the corner and the walls are rubble. The same thing happens with mine. Little openings in the ashlar blocks catch shadows and form narrow windows behind a bookcase. In place of the traditional quoins, there's a corner window in every alternative course." The peak of the house rises to bookend the unfinished end of the terrace and its unsightly mansard roof, added in the 1960s when design controls

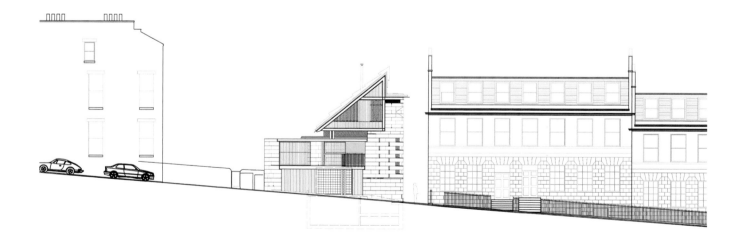

were weak. Quirky yet rigorous, and deeply rooted in the spirit of place, this original design was—quite predictably—rejected by the city's planning department, for fear it would create a precedent. Murphy was ready to appeal, but he had won the support of several city councillors and, to his surprise, they reversed the decision.

Then came the recession of 2008, and for more than four years Murphy lacked the funds to start construction. "The wait was useful because, now I've turned sixty, I'm not going to design another house, and the worst nightmare would be to move in and suddenly have a bright idea you should have had earlier," he says. "There are a thousand and one design decisions

within the envelope of a house, and in one as tightly planned as this, there's a knock-on effect whenever you move one element." When British-born Australian architect Glenn Murcutt came to stay, he approvingly called the house a Rubik's Cube.

The interior has nine distinct levels and non-repetitive vertical circulation. Murphy was inspired by the staircases in Scottish tower houses and the *Raumplan* of Adolf Loos's Villa Müller outside Prague. Other influences are in evidence. Murphy's love of Carlo Scarpa appears in the collage of the street facade and a tiled roof terrace that pays homage to the Querini Stampalia palace in Venice. Mirrors are used in the way Sir John Soane employed them, to trick

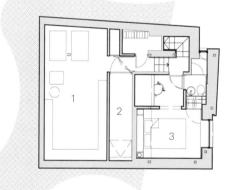

Plans of the basement and ground floor (top row), and of the first and second floors (bottom row). Key:

1 storeroom/plant room
2 log store
3 bedroom
4 utility room
5 entrance
6 study
7 roof terrace
8 living room
9 kitchen
10 dining room

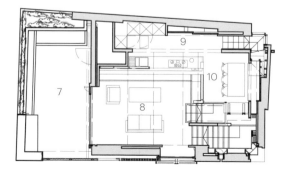

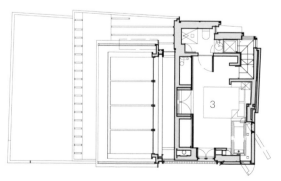

Mechanized shutters swing up to admit breezes and vent hot air in the living room (opposite) and master bedroom (below). The gold tiles in the courtyard (page 41, top right) are a tribute to Carlo Scarpa's interventions at the Palazzo Querini Stampalia in Venice.

the eye and enlarge tight spaces. But those references are assimilated; playfulness never lapses into pastiche.

The Dutch architect Aldo van Eyck said that a house should be both a bird's nest and a cave, and Murphy was eager to have *his* change its character with the seasons, from the dark winters to the summer months, when it stays light till midnight. A video on his website shows him opening flaps and sliding shutters, turning the house into an animate object, snugly enclosed or open to the sky. It conserves energy and nourishes the soul. Two large mechanized and well-insulated shutters, one in the living room and one in the master bedroom,

swing up to admit breezes and vent hot air. A geothermal well provides underfloor heating, and a computerized air circulation system takes warm air from the top of the house to the basement, where it is stored and released in the evening.

Hart Street House has won several awards, including the Royal Institute of British Architects' 2016 House of the Year. Murphy is gratified by the attention and the hope that it will bring him further commissions, but still more by the sensory pleasures the house affords. As he says, "There's nothing substantial I would change, but I'll polish off a few more small things over the next two decades."

# JENNIFER BENINGFIELD

# SWARTBERG HOUSE

# PRINCE ALBERT, SOUTH AFRICA

Building a house in London is almost as hard as dancing in a straitjacket. Every move is tightly regulated, and soaring property prices limit the size of most new projects. Jennifer Beningfield has been working within those constraints since she established Openstudio Architects in 2006, designing about forty houses and flats while sharing a small apartment with her publisher husband, David Jenkins. A financial settlement gave the couple the opportunity to build a second home in Beningfield's native South Africa, on a *tabula rasa* that allowed almost unlimited creative freedom.

The site is located between Prince Albert, a small town on the edge of the Karoo (an area of semi-desert), and the Swartberg Pass, a UNESCO World Heritage Site, 400 km from Cape Town. Beningfield and her husband had spent several vacations in the area, and were finally able to buy two hectares of farmland just outside the town. As they discussed what to build, Beningfield listed her wants: "A tower; a star-gazing terrace; a long pool in a garden; a cathedral space; ambiguity of inside and out; fun is important; strange scale; not an object." That cryptic checklist was as important as the concept sketches and plans in shaping a house that would have an organic relationship to its physical and climatic environment while meeting the owners' varied needs.

The first imperative was to respect the natural beauty of the landscape, with its farms, vineyards, and undulating horizon. "The house started out as a string of boxes," Beningfield recalls. "I didn't want a pure form—a long horizontal line against the backdrop of the mountains—but different volumes and spaces within a

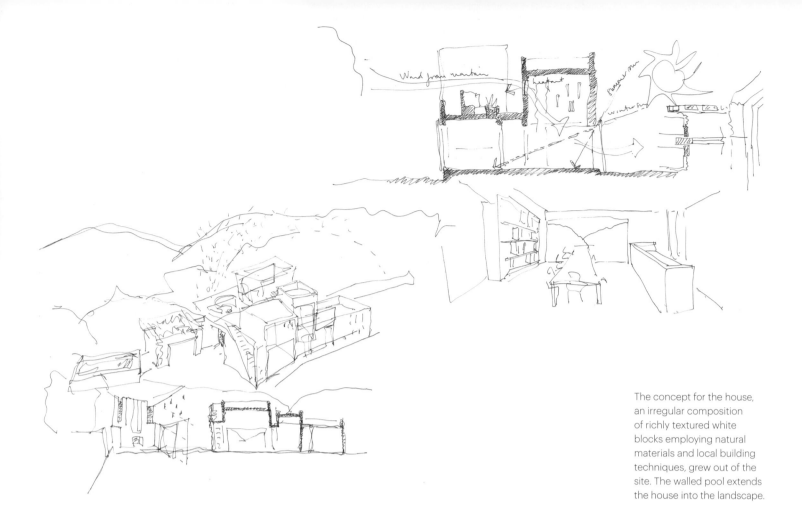

The concept for the house, an irregular composition of richly textured white blocks employing natural materials and local building techniques, grew out of the site. The walled pool extends the house into the landscape.

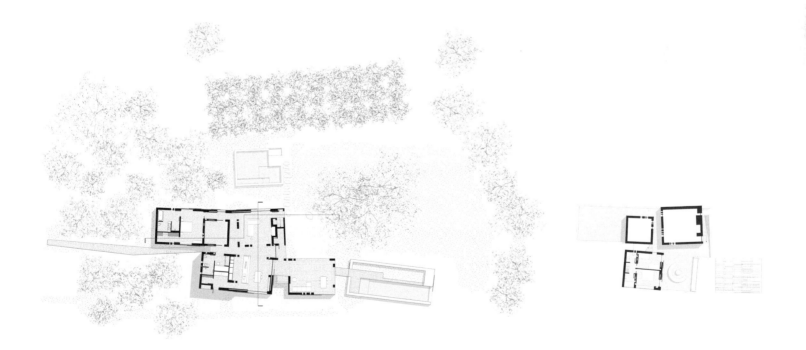

The living room (opposite) is a luminous, 5.7m cube, the master bathroom (right) is cave-like. The constant variation of scale and ceiling height gives the house its dynamic character.

unified whole. The spaces had a strong identity for me from the beginning, but the configuration changed as I moved the elements around and even considered an inwards-looking courtyard plan. In the final version, the rooms are oriented to frame specific views.

"The concept grew from the site and how people build in this area," Beningfield continues. "It's too remote to have access to sophisticated technology and precise detailing of the kind I take for granted in London. You can't get a flat plastered wall, for example." Other new residents had embarked on ambitious schemes that ended badly. Beningfield preferred to adapt the local vernacular of load-bearing brick walls, clad inside and out with rough-textured lime-washed plaster, and

cast-concrete beams. She was inspired by the first, stone-walled villa that Jørn Utzon built for his retirement on Mallorca, as well as the 1960s houses of architect Michael Sutton in Johannesburg.

The thick cavity walls and varied openings respond to the extremes of temperature and hot dry winds. On mild days and at night, the house can be opened up on three sides, leaving the solid west walls to baffle the sun. In the searing heat of summer, windows and external shutters are closed to keep the house cool during the day, and in winter the thermal mass of the house is warmed by the low sun. As a result, the house changes character with the seasons, and that makes its occupants more aware of what is going on around them, as well as eager to engage with the environment.

"I didn't want a house that felt too controlled or comfortable, but to have a looseness that would enable a different kind of behavior. Simple, but with layers of complexity that allow people to feel joyful."

Jennifer Beningfield

"When you design too tightly, you don't leave any room for accidents," says Beningfield. "I didn't want a house that felt too controlled or comfortable, but to have a looseness that would enable a different kind of behavior. Simple, but with layers of complexity that allow people to feel joyful."

The house has realized all of Beningfield's goals while also addressing the practical concerns of her husband, who, having previously worked in the office of Foster+Partners, played the role of critic. A mandatory height limit of 8m eliminated the tower, but their small daughter's bedroom feels very close to the starry sky her parents can contemplate from the roof terrace and its firepit. Walls of stone and greenery enclose the pool. The living room is a 5.7m cube, a cathedral-like space that leads into other generously proportioned rooms. Narrow slots cast patterns of light across the white walls, brick floors, and refined ash joinery.

There's a constant feeling of surprise in the varied scale of the different rooms, the alternation of brilliance and shadow, and the way in which a shutter opens to reveal a distant peak, a windmill, or a tree outlined against the sky: tightly framed natural landscapes that double as artworks.

Friends who come to stay and strangers who lease the house while the couple are away experience some of the same delight that not only draws Beningfield back to her homeland, but also renews her passion for the art and emotion of architecture.

# THOM MAYNE

# NOHO

# LOS ANGELES

From the day he cofounded Morphosis, Thom Mayne has delighted in complexity, talking about his architecture in the same tone of breathless urgency that Martin Scorsese brings to his analysis of cinema. One struggles to keep up with the words, but the bold gestures of his buildings never fail to excite.

In contrast to the provocative structures for which Morphosis are best known, Mayne's new house is an enigma, half buried in a sloping corner site. He dubbed it NOHO (No House), because dense plantings will eventually conceal it from the street and its suburban neighbors. Already, pink bougainvillea clads the retaining wall to the north, a hedge screens the house to the west, and a row of olive trees rises above a courtyard and stepped herb garden to the east. King palms flank the street entry to the south, providing shade and privacy.

American author Ray Bradbury lived in the house that formerly occupied this site, and his memory is honored by quotations laser-cut into a corten steel gate. Words are overlaid in the gate, which opens onto a wooden bridge spanning a lap pool. An automated glass panel slides back, and one descends into the subterranean living area to discover not a realm of shadows but a luminous vision of Eden. Pocketing glass sliders open onto the pool and landscaped courtyards, and light flows in from three sides and above. There are no barriers, and the only interior door is to the guest bathroom.

It's a house of voids and vistas, with a long east–west axis (emphasized by a projecting steel beam) and five shifts of level between the wine cellar and the cantilevered guest wings. Its 230 sq m of enclosed space occupy only 18 percent of the permitted volume, in contrast to the mega-mansions that are destroying the character of similar communities in Southern California, but the house is precisely tailored to the needs and desires of a busy professional couple.

A bridge spans the pool to the glass sliders of the entry (previous page). Plantings fill a sunken forecourt (above), and a laser-cut corten steel gate celebrates Ray Bradbury, who once lived at this address (above, right).

Soon after they married, Thom and Blythe Mayne remodeled a small house in the beachfront community of Santa Monica and raised two sons there. "Over thirty-four years," explains Thom, "we found a balance in the space and all the things we brought to it. Now the boys have left home, we tried to bring some of the same features to the new house, showering in the garden, and putting a built-in couch beside the tub so I can sit and chat with Blythe while she's bathing. It's about the ritualization of domestic routines."

Inspiration came from vacation retreats in the Mexican countryside, where one spends even more time outdoors than in Southern California. As a fledgling architect, Mayne

was deeply impressed by the Renaissance Villa Giulia in Rome—a modest building in a big garden—and by the spatial excitement of Ray Kappe's house in Los Angeles (see page 168). "From the beginning, I wanted to maximize the wall of landscape," he explains. "Carving out the earth was the first step, and the house kept getting pushed lower, which allowed us to expand the footprint underground. The biggest, lightest space is in the deepest, furthest corner of the site. It's all about connectivity—the opposite of classical stasis. I love the notion of radical contrasts and conflicts and unexpected occurrences."

The house gains added distinction from its materiality. Green aluminum cladding

Plans (right, from top)
of the subterranean level,
the main level, the upper
level, and the guest wing
and roof. Key:

1 plant room
2 cellar
3 swimming pool
4 studio
5 carport
6 bathroom
7 entry gate
8 kitchen
9 dining room
10 outdoor fireplace
11 outdoor shower
12 bedroom
13 library
14 communal room

Below, a longitudinal
cross-section and one
of the architect's early
sketches of the house.

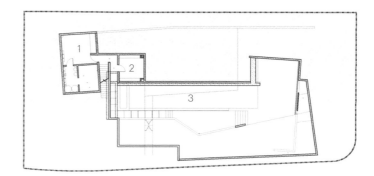

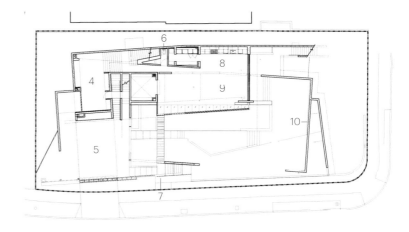

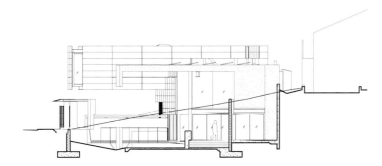

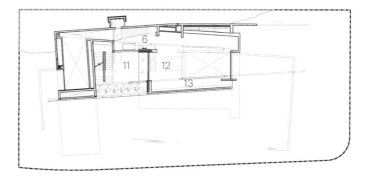

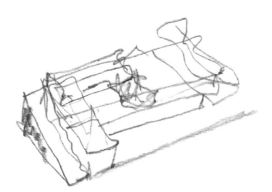

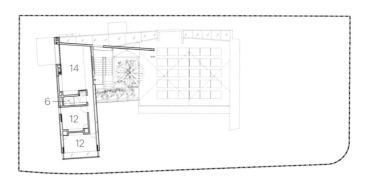

Trees screen the house from the street and neighbors (opposite). The living room (right) has a sleeping area above it, while a skylight illuminates the tapered staircase (below).

panels, with a pattern of flat and tilted discs that catch the light, were borrowed from Morphosis' building on the Cornell Tech campus in New York. Ceilings of Douglas fir plywood conceal LEDs, sprinklers, and speakers behind a pattern of pierced openings, as well as adding warmth to the exposed concrete walls and floors. Light switches are hidden behind openings in wall panels, and every detail has been meticulously designed.

Metal artisan Tom Farrage has contributed functional steel sculptures, from the hearth to the buttresses that support the mezzanine sleeping area and its headboard. Floors have radiant heating and the house is cooled by cross-ventilation. Net-zero energy consumption is the goal, with rooftop solar panels and

the recycling of gray water complementing the thermal mass.

"Pushback from a client is essential if a house is to have soul," says Blythe. "I never add a line to his lines; I just talk about the feeling of it. The kitchen is where our family gathers. Thom initially designed a linear space and I said no. It was completely changed. I insisted we take the roof off the guest shower, and use a movable skylight that mostly stays open so friends can take showers in the rain as we do. Heaters are for wimps."

Open and compact, raw yet hedonistic, NOHO is a model for city living in Southern California, as the Case Study Houses were six decades ago.

# JOHN WARDLE

# SHEARERS' QUARTERS

# BRUNY ISLAND, AUSTRALIA

Like many Australians, John Wardle has a deep affection for the land. In his case, it prompted him to seek a retreat from the routine of his flourishing practice in Melbourne. Memories of a boyhood trip to Bruny Island, a skinny strip of land off Tasmania, encouraged him to look for a foothold there. In 2002, he and his wife, Susan, bought a 440 hectare sheep farm along with a cottage that Captain James Kelly had built on the island in the 1840s.

For the first decade, the couple spent weekends and school holidays in Kelly's cottage, planting trees and rejuvenating the landscape. It worked well for the family, but there was little room for guests—especially when, once a year for two weeks, the sheep shearers would share their quarters. Knowing he would need a long time to restore the old cottage, Wardle decided to build a second, 130 sq m house for family and friends on the site of a shearing shed that had burned down in the 1980s.

"We couldn't afford to build it for many years, so I had plenty of time to study the site and think what to do," says Wardle. "It's a speculation on what was once there, with two different roof forms—the narrow skillion [monopitch] and wide gable—both agricultural staples. That creates a fascinating geometry, which looks simple but is amazingly complex."

At the last moment, after the scheme had been drawn up and permissions granted, Wardle moved it 4 m so that the inset verandah would line up with the verandah of the cottage, as well as the fall of the land

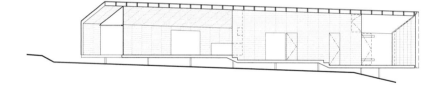

A deceptively simple shelter of recycled wood and corrugated galvanized iron draws on the Australian rural vernacular, but the siting and geometries were meticulously calculated. A retreat for family and friends, it is home to sheep shearers for two weeks a year.

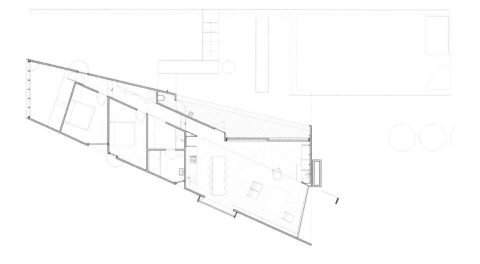

to the south. It was to be an indoor–outdoor gathering place that would frame views of coast and farmland.

From this basic program, Wardle devised a house that is tactile and precisely scaled, winning more awards than any of his larger projects. "It was a challenge for the builder, but luckily I was the client and could take my time," he says. "And we had a remarkable carpenter with a fine arts degree." Thin, steel screw piles support the house an average of 60 cm above the ground, so no foundations were required. The wood frame is clad in corrugated galvanized iron—a ubiquitous material in Australia—which Glenn Murcutt has used with rare artistry.

Within the spacious living area, two bedrooms and a bunkroom are organized on a 7 m grid that aligns all the windows, doors, walls, and joinery. Most of the interior is lined with *Pinus macrocarpa*, scavenged from old rural windbreaks. The floors are of yellow stringybark, while the bedrooms

are lined with recycled apple crates. Wardle found this cut timber stacked in the storage sheds of orchards that had gone out of business in the 1970s. The chimney was constructed from old handmade clay bricks and echoes the three external chimneys of the cottage.

The use of recycled materials contributes to the sustainability of the house, which is nestled low to shelter it from prevailing winds. Openable vents and a louvered breezeway provide cross-ventilation in summer; double glazing and high-performance insulation reduce heat loss in winter. Rainwater is collected for drinking, toilets, and showers, while waste water is treated on-site and used to irrigate the plantings of native trees. Water is solar-heated, and there is a wood-burning stove for chilly months.

This is a house that engages the senses and the landscape, as well as extending the history of the site. The dining table, where

everyone gathers at the end of the day, looks out to the shearing shed at the top of the hill. The aroma and texture of the timber give the house a living presence, which delighted Finnish architect Juhani Pallasmaa when he came to stay. There's poetry in the play of light, especially at sunset, when the last rays stream in through the wide openings, turning the wood to gold. The acoustics are so good that the living room doubles as a performance space and has hosted chamber music recitals.

To get to the house, one has to take a flight from Melbourne to Hobart, a 45-minute drive to Kettering to catch a 30-minute ferry to Bruny Island, and then another half-hour drive to the property. A resident manager looks after the farm year-round, but Wardle takes his family there at least once a month and more in summer. He invites his staff for annual retreats, and two years ago he helped create a series of art installations, in collaboration with a specialist tree cutter, an arborist, a stone mason, and a carpenter. "It's such a pleasure to spend time there," says Wardle, "and it's taught me to appreciate the craft skills that are available for my other buildings."

# HANS VAN HEESWIJK

# RIETEILAND HOUSE

# AMSTERDAM

"I wanted a house that would maximize light and views, and be as spacious as possible," says Dutch architect Hans van Heeswijk. Twenty-five years earlier, he had refurbished an apartment building in Amsterdam South and might have continued living there; however, his new wife, Natascha Drabbe, had found it oppressively dark. Having grown up in the countryside and lived in the Van Schijndel House (see page 172), she craved a sense of openness.

An opportunity soon arose. Plots of land on one of the artificial islands that make up IJburg, a residential district a short cycle ride to the east of Amsterdam, were offered for sale in a lottery, and Van Heeswijk and his wife were the first to build there. The city mandates modern architecture in new developments while preserving the integrity of its historic legacy, and that allowed the architect to express himself freely.

Van Heeswijk had been fantasizing about a residence that would have the simplicity and varied room heights of Le Corbusier's Citrohan House or that of the Eameses. He quickly sketched a three-story cube that was shielded from the street with perforated aluminum panels, but which opened up on the other three sides. Venetian blinds can be lowered to shade the well-insulated walls of glass; the third floor is cut away to provide a terrace that overlooks the water and a public park to the west. It's a house for all seasons: a snug refuge from wind and rain, as well as at night; a canvas on

Venetian blinds can be lowered to shade well-insulated walls of glass, while the third floor is cut away to provide a terrace that overlooks the water. From the living room, one can view the full height of the house.

When the glass walls slide
open, the house becomes
a giant pergola (opposite).
The kitchen/dining area is
double height, the staircase
triple, the living room double,
and the bedroom single.
Looking up from the foot of
the central staircase, one can
view all three levels (above).

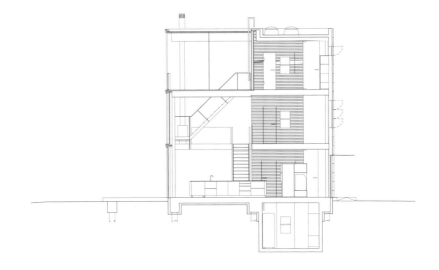

Plans (left, from bottom) of the ground, first and second floors.

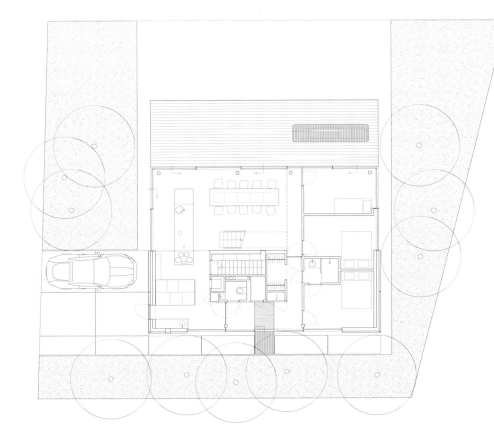

which the sun casts moving patterns of light and shade; and a giant pergola when the expanses of glass slide open. "The entry front looks rather austere—people ask if it's an electrical power station—but when they see the other facades, they think we must be living in a display window," says Drabbe. Reflections off the glass and blinds at night give the owners all the privacy they need in this quiet neighborhood. The expansive windows of seventeenth-century merchants' houses, innovative in their day, may have prompted similar concerns.

"Traditional houses have separate rooms opening off a corridor," says Van Heeswijk. "Here, everything is open—the ultimate spatial quality. I left out as many inner walls as I could to achieve a continuous flow and never have the feeling of being

locked in. And I wanted spatial variety. The kitchen/dining area is double height, the staircase three, living room two, bedroom one—an alternation that gives the house a very relaxed quality. It's designed around our daily activities, of eating, sitting, entertaining, and sleeping.

"I created every element in the house as a functional artwork," he continues, "from built-ins to door handles. I didn't need to do that, but it was an awful lot of fun. Favorite pieces of furniture, like Corbu's Petit Confort armchair, [Gerrit] Rietveld's Zig-Zag chair, and the Eames Aluminum Group, serve as strategically placed sculpture, so we don't need to hang art on the walls." The architect limited the palette of materials to the basics. Floors and ceiling are gray concrete, walls are white stucco, staircases raw steel. The core is clad in strips of wenge wood to absorb sound, and is detailed as a piece of furniture with rounded corners. As you walk around, invisible doors open to reveal service and storage spaces. "Hans is fond of gray and a specific tone of white," says Drabbe, "so I added colors within the core." Toilets are apple green, walk-in closets yellow. One side reveals accents of blue, another red. At night, strips of red glow through the windows as though from an open fire.

A geothermal pump, rooftop solar panels, and radiantly heated and cooled floors assure a high level of sustainability, along with external louvers and interior screens. Because the area was raised from the sea, the soil is still salty and many trees won't grow here, but reeds flourish and other plantings will be added. The crisp geometry

of the house dissolves in the ripples of the nearby water, and the glass facades mirror the passing clouds as though this were a Dutch landscape painting. Van Heeswijk has realized his goal of creating a sharp contrast between the house and its setting—what Richard Neutra called "the machine in the garden."

Rieteiland House was widely published in the Netherlands, and a client asked Van Heeswijk to design a glass farmhouse with a Miesian plan. The contractor introduced another client, for whom the architect has designed a white villa in Eindhoven. Nevertheless, Van Heeswijk's firm remains focused on the public and institutional buildings for which it is best known.

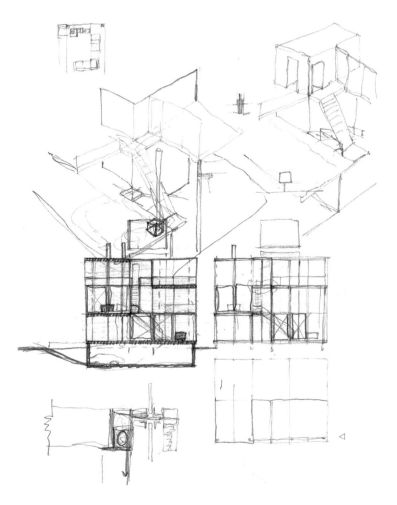

# ANTÓN GARCÍA-ABRIL & DÉBORA MESA

# HEMEROSCOPIUM, MADRID

# CYCLOPEAN, BROOKLINE, MASSACHUSETTS

A visionary husband-and-wife team have designed two houses for themselves to test their ideas and serve as manifestos on how to use prefabrication to create inspiring and affordable places to live. "If you stick to the building code," insists García-Abril, "you will produce coded architecture. It's essential to push the envelope." That resolve produced the Hemeroscopium, which was built from massive prestressed concrete beams on a former tennis court outside Madrid, and the Cyclopean, which uses styrofoam beams and provides the couple with a base while they are teaching at MIT.

The Hemeroscopium is an astonishing spectacle, largely because the massive structure is fully exposed. "It started as a research project—an opportunity to realize an experiment that was in our heads," explains Mesa. "We wanted to explore the logistics of creating a structure in which beams would be stacked asymmetrically to achieve a balance." They visited a factory where beams are made for large-scale civil projects, hoping to obtain rejects like the one they had seen lying beside a road. These were judged unsafe, so they ordered seven of specific lengths, cast from existing molds, with additional reinforcement.

It took the in-house engineer at the couple's Ensamble Studio a year to calculate the stresses, but the structure was erected in

Hemeroscopium combines mass and transparency in a construction of precast concrete beams tied together with steel rods and counterbalanced with a block of granite.

only seven days—as a helix of beams tied together with steel rods, and crowned at the point of equilibrium with a 20 tonne block of granite. This is a visible expression of the force of gravity and a physical counterweight to the beams, which enclose a courtyard and the free-flowing interiors. A lap pool is cantilevered out from the master bedroom. "It's fantastic to be in a fully transparent space within a monumental scale and to enjoy the vistas within and outside the house," says García-Abril. "We still have the house, but it's only 200 sq m, and now we have four children it's too small for our needs."

A second opportunity to give form to their ideas came when the couple relocated to the United States. Appalled by the price of property in Boston, they settled for the cheapest they could find: a trio of domestic garages in the residential

suburb of Brookline. This became the podium for a loft space that appears to be the polar opposite of its predecessor: a plain cube of metal-ribbed cement board with a ribbon of glass on the street facade. The challenge was to build atop the garages without requiring additional support, so they designed a structure of seven styrofoam beams, clad in cement board and edged in metal, that would contain beds, kitchen, bathroom, and built-in furniture. These were fabricated in a Madrid factory, shipped to Boston in a container, and speedily assembled on-site. The entire 230 sq m house weighs less than one of the concrete beams from their previous project.

"With Hemeroscopium, we were using existing technology and decontextualizing it," explains Mesa. "With Cyclopean, we are creating a new technology by combining

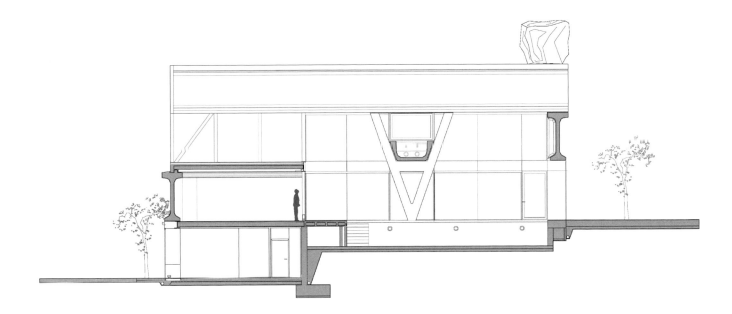

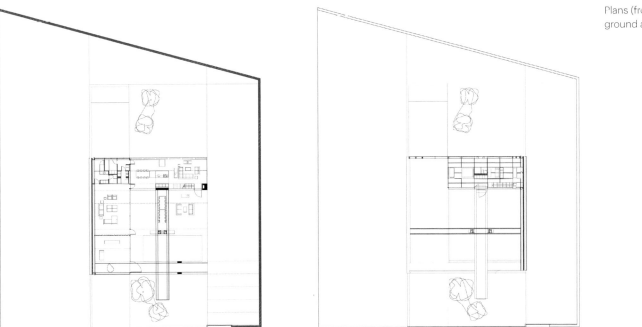

Plans (from far left) of the ground and first floors.

Within the monumental frame of Hemeroscopium is an intimate dining room (above) and a master bedroom that opens onto a cantilevered lap pool (opposite).

elements that are typically used for insulation, not as structure." The beams are stacked, forming what appears to be a solid wall. Traditional houses surround the site on three sides, and there the openings are small. The garages have been remodeled to serve as a master suite and home office, and will soon be clad in creeper climbing an outer layer of galvanized mesh. Upstairs is a single lofty volume with services ranged around the perimeter, and steps leading up to a mezzanine gallery and roof terrace. This acts as a gathering place for family and friends, as well as the children's bedroom and playroom.

Surprisingly for such a radical project, Cyclopean sailed through the approvals process. "We told the building department that the house was pre-manufactured without going into details of what or where," recalls García-Abril. "They seemed less interested in the structure than in the

mechanical systems—the inspector's chief concern was the size of the shower nozzle." Adds Mesa, "The construction process has an artistic value—from the creation of the elements in a distant factory to the choreography of the assembly to reduce the number of movements during construction."

Poetry and functionality are fused in these houses. In Greek mythology, Hemeroscopium is where the sun sets— a place that exists only in the imagination. "Cyclopean," meanwhile, is a reference to the one-eyed giant in Homer's *Odyssey* and the long journey taken by the house to its final destination. Its success advances the goal of Ensamble to integrate research, practice, and architectural education. It also has the potential, if other building departments are as enlightened as that of Boston, to generate affordable housing.

"If you stick to the building code,
you will produce coded architecture.
It's essential to push the envelope."

Antón García-Abril

Cyclopean rises from
a trio of domestic garages,
remodeled to serve as
a master suite and home
studio. This podium supports
a lightweight assembly of
board-clad styrofoam beams
that enclose a double-height
family room with fold-out
beds for the children.

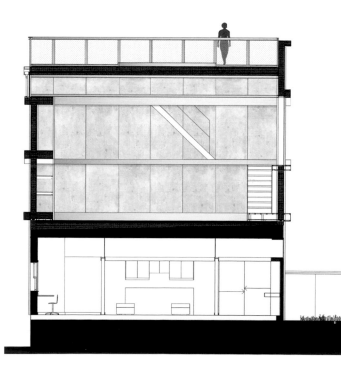

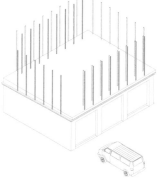

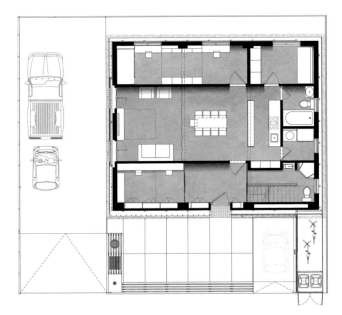

Plans (from far left) of the ground and first floors.

# TODD SAUNDERS

# VILLA S

# BERGEN, NORWAY

Growing up in Newfoundland, Todd Saunders saw few prospects on home ground and moved to Norway, where he could find clients for his residential practice and continue to enjoy the great outdoors. Work took precedence, and after fixing up a trio of flats close to his office in Bergen, he began searching for a site where he could build a house for his family.

Saunders bought a former park in a garden suburb that architect Leif Grung had designed in the 1930s, but then discovered, as he cleared the trees, that the land was boggy. "I took a 3m length of rebar, pushed it into the earth, and it disappeared," he recalls. "An engineer advised me to dig it out and fill it with rocks. It was a rough start."

The architect sketched many different schemes before deciding to base his design on a dialogue between wants and needs. Bergen is one of the rainiest places in Europe, and that suggested covered spaces where the family could be outdoors but stay dry.

Tired of scrambling up and down stairs, from one floor to the next, Saunders resolved to put all the living spaces on one level in a linear block raised above the ground. This would allow him to drive in and unload under cover, as well as providing his two young daughters with somewhere to play. Like its neighbors, the house faces west to draw in whatever light there is, and every room is lit from front and back.

Restraint and simplicity were the guiding principles—how to strip a house to its essentials without skimping on materials. The concept evolved into three strokes: a horizontal bar cantilevered off a vertical stack and a cross-axial bar of storage. That minimized the foundations. The vertical element contains the staircase, which leads up from the entry and a room where the children can watch television, through the main floor to a third-level library that opens onto a roof terrace.

The steel frame was clad with boards of black wood, to blend in with the trees and provide a contrast with the customary Norwegian palette of white, red, and yellow. The underside, however, is white, to emphasize the volume of the block.

"In Norway," Saunders explains, "you don't need a design review if you stay within the building regulations, but local residents can stop the project. Luckily,

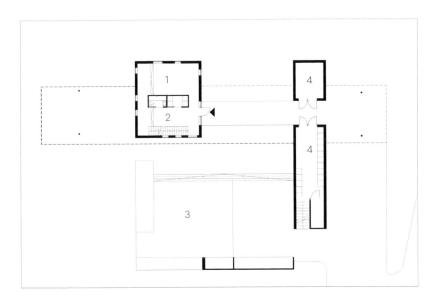

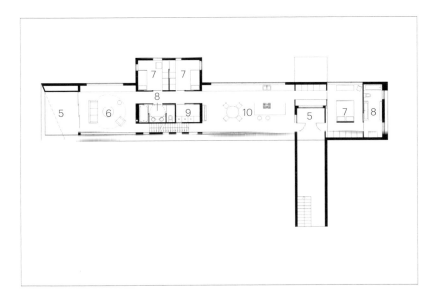

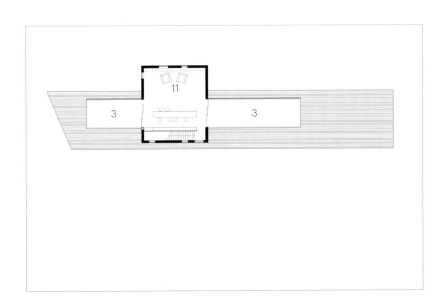

Plans (from top) of the
ground, first and second
floors. Key:

1  TV room
2  entrance
3  outside area
4  storage
5  balcony
6  living room
7  bedroom
8  bathroom
9  laundry
10  kitchen
11  library

Living spaces are tightly concentrated on the middle level of the house. The kitchen/dining room (right) can be accessed by steps from the enclosed entry hall or from the firewood stack in the front yard. A sculptural staircase leads up to the library (opposite).

I had got to know my fourteen neighbors while I was prepping the site and showed the drawings to each of them. Many had spent all their lives in the modern dwellings Grung designed and that made them willing to approve mine. The park had become a dumping ground, so they saw my house as an enhancement to the neighborhood. And knowing I had a reputation in the city, they trusted me to build it well.

"Because I'm a foreigner," Saunders continues, "I see Norwegian culture in a fresh light, and approach design in an intuitive way without preconceptions. I found inspiration in the work of Grung and other architects of that era, using the kind of wood cladding that contemporary architects have moved away from. The interior was planned meticulously, drawing on my experience of designing other houses." All the working parts of the house, including the laundry, are grouped tightly together. A cube in the entry conceals jackets and muddy boots. The library is a place to read, but also to draw and make models.

The master bathroom (above). The living room (opposite, top) opens onto a covered porch, and the library (opposite, bottom) is flanked by roof terraces that can be enjoyed on rare sunny days.

Saunders worked with his favorite contractors, who gave him a good price and use the house in their advertising. Quality is built in: the Danish floorboards are 5 cm thick, 45 cm wide, and up to 14 m long. The window company he had worked with for fifteen years had just developed triple-glazed panels, and he was able to use a new insulation product. He drilled down 170 m to provide geothermal heat for underfloor warming, and when he adds solar panels to heat the water, there will be no electricity bill.

For interior furnishings, Saunders summoned his good friend Hannes Wingate from Portland, Oregon, who helped select unique pieces from

Denmark, a piano from a German craftsman in Bergen, and a green sofa from Donna Wilson in Scotland, as well as reupholstering furniture that Saunders had inherited.

"I sit out on the covered kitchen balcony even when it's pouring and, on the thirty days a year when the sun shines, we use the roof terrace and imagine we have gone to the Mediterranean," says Saunders, who is currently a single father. "It's also a showcase. Clients who come here can visualize what I do. Seven of them have commissioned houses that are now under construction."

# JIM OLSON

# LONGBRANCH

# PUGET SOUND, WASHINGTON STATE

# "When I'm drawing floor plans, I imagine myself sitting in different places and thinking about vistas and sunlight coming through the trees."

## Jim Olson

"I've never been jealous of my clients' homes, which are a hundred times more elaborate than mine," says Jim Olson. "I would rather live in my cabin than anything I've done for someone else. Each of the other houses is about a client's dreams and aspirations, and I help them realize those. This is much more modest, but it didn't have to be; it's how we are. The larger houses are about entertaining— almost like civic buildings; ours is a retreat, hiding out in the woods."

As a founding partner of Olson Kundig in Seattle, the architect has designed more than two hundred houses over fifty years; his own weekend retreat spans his entire adult life. While still a first-year architecture student, Olson built a bunkhouse alongside his parents' home on land his grandfather had bought. In 1981 came three cabins— for living, sleeping, and bathing—on a diagonal axis linked by walkways. Twenty years later, he added a new living room and a roof for shelter. The most recent and

ambitious expansion comprises a new master suite, a courtyard, and a library for his wife, Katherine, with two guest rooms tucked in below, where the land falls away. That increased the floor area to 225 sq m and created a unified sequence of rooms running parallel to the waterfront below. Olson describes it as "a series of boxes under one roof."

"At first it was about adding space," he recalls. "Later, as we got older, it was more about creature comforts—not having to walk to the bathroom on a rain-slicked deck and sparing guests from sleeping on couches in the living room. The philosophy was the same, but the level of refinement was higher. It was feedback from our practice: the desire to create unpretentious but beautifully crafted spaces for others, and now for ourselves."

Olson was in no rush to make these changes, preferring instead to think them through at leisure. He had dreamed of

The house has grown incrementally over fifty years, facing out to the water and backing onto a forest. Two guest rooms are tucked in below the main floor, where the ground falls away.

103

The master suite was based on an idea Olson had sketched two years earlier. The older parts of the house are of simple wood-frame construction, but the bedroom required steel beams to support the cantilevered floor and roof planes.

Site plan showing the main
level of the house. Key:

1   bathroom
2   bedroom
3   courtyard
4   den
5   utility room
6   kitchen
7   dining room
8   living room
9   gym

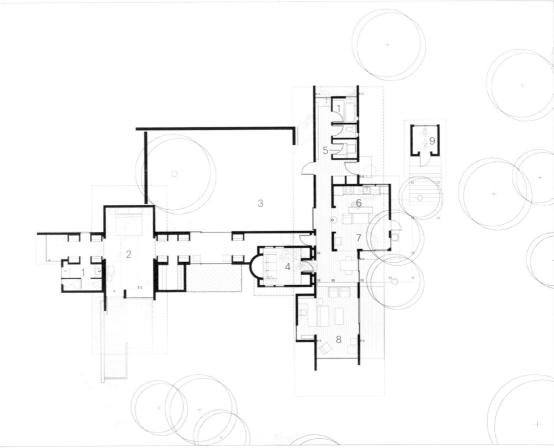

the new living room for ten years before starting construction, and the master suite was based on an idea he had sketched on a trip to Hawaii two years earlier. Before deciding on the final plan, Olson worked on some alternatives, turning the new wing to get a better view, then going in the other direction. What seemed most logical was to extend it on the axis of the previous house. He wanted his wife to feel cradled, with a view to the water, and not unprotected in the middle of a forest.

"When I'm drawing floor plans," explains Olson, "I imagine myself sitting in different places and thinking about vistas and sunlight coming through the trees. The bed is cozy and secluded, and the deck that

extends out puts you in the tree tops; you feel like a little bird."

The earlier stages of the house are of simple wood-frame construction, but the bedroom required steel beams to support the cantilevered floor and roof planes. The local builder rented a small crane, and Olson went out every weekend to check on progress, dream up further refinements, and leave little sketches for the builder to pick up on Monday.

The house backs onto forest, where Olson feels entirely at home, but his wife asked for a courtyard that could be illuminated at night so she was not looking out to a dark void. These additions and a linear

library are seamlessly linked to the older parts of the property, which retain their informal, weathered character. Trays of shells and a few low-key artworks are the only decoration. Olson designed a simple plank chair to complement the woodsy interiors and plain modern furnishings, and a sprinkler system was installed throughout the house, which is a long way from the nearest fire station.

"It's a house that isn't about itself, but what it does," says the architect. "It allows you to be as close as possible to the outdoors without having to be in the rain. When you do things for yourself, you put yourself in the position of the client. It helps me to understand how clients feel,

making a decision before they can see the finished product. No amount of sketches, models, and computer renderings can prepare you for what it's going to be like. If it's two people, you have to be sure that both are getting most of what they want. My wife said she didn't want to be an innkeeper, so the guest rooms have their own entrance and a kitchen. That lets me entertain clients downstairs.

"Coming here," concludes Olson, "I'm drawn to nature and the trees and the quiet. And when I go back to the city, I feel energized."

# MAURICIO PEZO & SOFIA VON ELLRICHSHAUSEN

## CIEN

## CONCEPCIÓN, CHILE

Sofia met Pezo while studying in Buenos Aires, and married him soon after they had established their small studio in Concepción, 500 km to the south of their peers in Santiago. At first it was hard: each wanted to take the lead, and they would fight. Now, however, they take turns in advancing their ideas and playing critic, until they've resolved their differences and can work harmoniously together. "We want our buildings to be timeless and not draw attention to themselves," says Sofia. "We only accept projects that give us a sufficient measure of creative freedom. Every house is a learning experience, to explore something we haven't done before, but we don't change rapidly or quickly exhaust topics."

Cien, the live–work space that Sofia and Pezo built for themselves, is a proud demonstration of their independent spirit: a slender, five-level tower of bush-hammered concrete rising from a podium of living space, with a workshop in the basement. It's named for the height of the podium, 100 m above sea level, and it hugs a narrow, sloping site. Six years earlier, the couple had built Poli, a cube of rough shuttered concrete on a rocky headland overlooking the Pacific. That serves as a weekend retreat and as an experiment: a complex of interlocking geometries that seems to be carved from a solid block, like an Eduardo Chillida sculpture. Irregular, deep-set openings frame tiny vistas of rock and ocean, while light spills over the formwork boards that line the walls.

Cien is more refined than Poli, thanks to a higher level of skill in construction, although an earthquake halted work as the podium was being completed, and the concrete of the tower contains a smaller agregate. The design began with cardboard and concrete models, exploring a geometrical concept. First, a 6 m square was divided by an asymmetrical cross; this division was then varied twelve times in the floor plan of the house. The windows puncture the facades from within, reinforcing visual connections. Their size and height correspond to the placement of a table, or where someone might be sitting or standing. The interiors are as rigorous as those of Le Corbusier's Couvent de la Tourette. Walls are clad in white or pale-gray painted boards, and the living spaces have wood floors. Elsewhere, the concrete is exposed and galvanized steel frames hold the windows in place.

Each part of the house has its own distinct role. The basement is where the couple create and store their own paintings, which have steadily evolved over the years. From the entrance, one steps down from the kitchen to the dining room to the sparely furnished living area, through arched openings that create a lively rhythm. The master bedroom above opens onto terraces atop the podium. Pezo bought the giant cypress to the rear as a birthday present for Sofia, and they now regard it as a natural extension of the house. Wooden staircases spiral upward, one to the master suite and guest bedroom above, the other to the studio spaces on the upper floors.

"I question conventional notions of comfort," says Sofia. "Our house defies those conventions and yet I find it extremely comfortable. Going from my desk to my bathroom involves five flights of stairs, but I'm invigorated by the exercise and the fresh air of the terrace." Her husband agrees: "We don't make a distinction between our private and working lives," he says. "But there are other people who spend five days a week with us and we try to make a separation. Given the sedentary nature of our profession, it's good that we should escape from our desks.

"In a remote place like this," Pezo continues, "there are few potential clients. They are unsophisticated, their budgets are low; they are ordinary people who happen to like us." The architects welcome the opportunity to chip away at prejudices. "We've invited neighbors into Cien and they are astonished by how different it is from what they expected," says Sofia. "One said he had hated the house, but had now come around to liking it."

The couple accept the challenge of working on a small scale, one project at a time, as well as the rewards of building everything as though they were going to live there themselves. However, they enjoy greater freedom when they have only themselves to please. "Added volume," says Pezo, "is more important to us than the quality of construction—here, in Poli, and in the larger country house we are building at the foot of the Andes now that we are out of space in Cien. That's a choice you can rarely offer a client."

"I question conventional notions of comfort. Going from my desk to my bathroom involves five flights of stairs, but I'm invigorated by the exercise and the fresh air of the terrace."

Sofia von Ellrichshausen

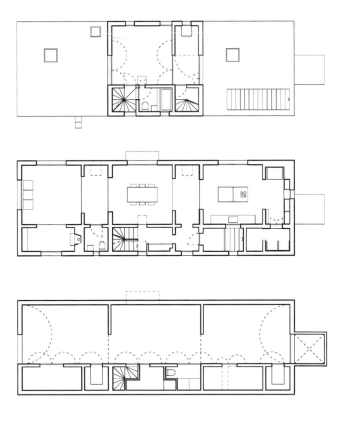

Plans (above, from bottom) of the basement, ground floor and first floor of Cien.

# HELLE SCHRÖDER & MARTIN JANEKOVIC

## NO WALLS

## BERLIN

The trauma of the wall that sundered Berlin for three decades has become a distant memory for most residents of the city, although its few remains are heavily promoted to tourists and school groups. As partners in the firm of XTH-Berlin, Helle Schröder and her former husband, Martin Janekovic, bought an inexpensive site on the east side of where the wall once ran.

Before the architects could build there, the authorities decided to preserve a surviving fragment of the concrete barrier and turn the adjoining land into a memorial park. Schröder leased a site from the owner of property set further back and designed three four-story houses in a row of five, reserving the middle one for herself and her two daughters. Each has a different facade

treatment, but they come together as a single block, acting as a foil to both the park and the colorful new apartments that have risen on the west side of the former divide.

The location is fraught with emotion. Steel posts mark the line of the wall. In what was once the DDR security zone, an elliptical chapel has replaced a church that was demolished to open up a clear line of fire from East to West. Bronze markers trace the course of escape tunnels that were dug under the wall; another tunnel was cut at an angle by the Stasi to intercept them. The park is thronged during the day, so Schröder installed a fringe of canvas straps at ground and third levels to block the gaze of visitors in the park while allowing views out. In contrast to its fairly conventional neighbors, the floors of Schröder's house

Longitudinal cross-section
(below, right). Key:

1  terrace
2  kitchen/dining area
3  bedroom
4  sitting area
5  reading area
6  bathroom
7  music room
8  play area/storage

are masked by steel girders, but nothing on the facade prepares one for the radical configuration of the interior.

"I hadn't considered living in a terrace house," says Schröder, "and the design wasn't thought out long in advance. It's all about space and light." The house rises 12 m from a trapezoidal lot of 118 sq m. The shallow depth pulls in light and air from front and back, and a central staircase links seven levels, with more light coming from above. All levels are open, except for the two concrete structures of tilted slabs that contain the bedrooms, yet these too can be opened when they are not in use. They span the fire walls to either side, which are cross-braced by the steel girders. The verticality is a response to the confined site

and an expression of the relaxed lifestyle of the owner, while offering a diversity of internal perspectives. A first-time visitor can feel disoriented, as though having to navigate one of M. C. Escher's impossible staircases, and it was a big leap from apartment living for Schröder. But it has proved a perfect fit for her and her two daughters, both of whom have grown up in this unique living environment. And one soon comes to appreciate the ingenuity of a house that offers such a teasing mix of openness and enclosure, shared and private spaces, which reveal themselves from behind curtains and moving planes.

Fair-faced concrete is fully exposed and the side walls are plastered. The floors are covered with pinewood planks, the stairs

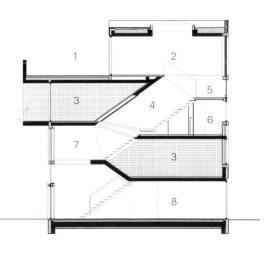

Large counterbalanced wood panels can be raised or lowered to reveal or conceal the bedrooms. The central staircase links all seven levels of the house, with netting across the voids.

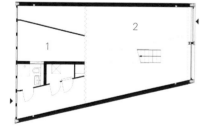 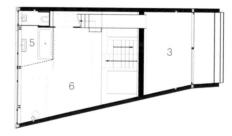

Plans (above, from left) of
the first/second, third/fourth,
and fifth/sixth levels. Key:

1   guest room
2   play area/storage
3   bedroom
4   music room
5   bathroom
6   sitting area

A bathroom can be curtained off from a living area (opposite, top). The kitchen/dining room opens onto a roof terrace (above), and supplies can be hoisted up by pulley from the rear entrance.

and joinery are whitened glue-laminated spruce, and the handrails are steel. Those spare surfaces provide a backdrop to the cheerful clutter in the children's rooms and the entry hall, which links the front and rear entrances; other spaces are minimally furnished with custom-designed built-ins. The ground floor contains a guest room, storage, and play space. Stair treads are set into planks and lead up to the first two bedrooms, which can be entered by raising large counterbalanced wood panels.

The switchback staircase continues up to a music room, sitting area, reading ledge, and a third bedroom with an open bathroom that can be curtained off. Above this, on the top floor, is a kitchen/dining area opening onto a rear terrace that overlooks a close of sixteen new town houses.

Inventive touches abound. A pulley can be used to hoist provisions up the rear facade. Nets are deployed across voids, as though for high-wire performers in a circus. A large skylight allows midday sun to penetrate to the lower levels, and can be opened to vent hot air. A heat pump warms panels throughout the house, and rainwater is collected and recycled for use in the toilets.

The name of this iconoclastic house is No Walls, a reference to its open plan and to the transformation of Berlin from a divided city to the vibrant capital of a reunified country, which is regaining some of the excitement it generated in the 1920s. Everywhere, creatives are leaving their mark; with No Walls, Schröder has made her contribution to this renaissance.

# PETER & THOMAS GLUCK

# TOWER HOUSE

# ULSTER COUNTY, NEW YORK STATE

In 1961, Peter Gluck bought a tumbledown 1820s farmhouse with 8 hectares of forested land on the edge of the Catskill State Park, and restored it as a weekend retreat. His son Thomas, now a partner in Gluck+, built the Bridge House for weekend guests, working hands-on as a carpenter before he went to architecture school. Peter added the Scholar's Library for his wife, Carol, a professor of Japanese history at Columbia, and collaborated with his son on the latest addition to the family compound.

Thomas took the lead in designing the Tower House, even before he moved back to New York with his wife and two small children. He placed it atop a steep rocky ridge overlooking the other structures. To minimize the footprint and maximize views, he conceived the house as a stack of small bedrooms supporting a spacious gathering area. That yielded an off-center T-form with a living room cantilevered from a steel frame and supported on one side by a "V" of slender columns. A grid of maple trees was planted to replace those that had been removed during construction, and the regularity of the plantings plays off the geometry of the tower. A 25 m long bridge links it to the upper level of the guest house, and a big lawn unites the three buildings below the ridge.

"I was in Minneapolis when the project began," recalls Thomas. "I sketched and made models and together we pushed the design along. Because we were architects building for ourselves, we could create a design that focused on the essentials without compromise. It would be hard to sell a client on the idea of putting the living room atop a switchback staircase."

"Because we were architects building for ourselves, we could create a design that focused on the essentials without compromise. It would be hard to sell a client on the idea of putting the living room atop a switchback staircase."

Thomas Gluck

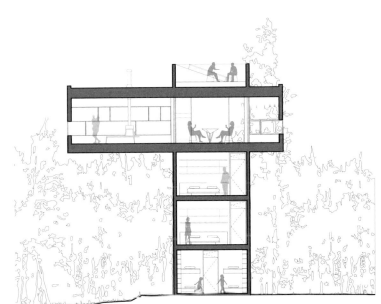
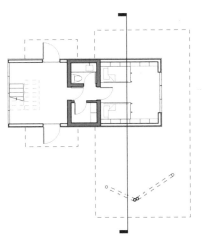
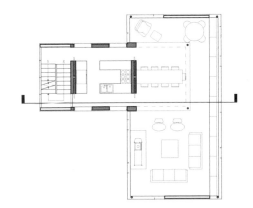

Another bold move was to clad the entire building in a taut curtain wall of clear and green back-painted glass, rather than mimicking the woodsiness of the site as most clients would have wanted to do. It's counterintuitive, but the man-made form dissolves into reflections. In form and in surface, the house becomes a part of the forest.

It helped that Gluck+ is a design–build firm. "We were able to buy the glass and equipment from a subcontractor we've worked with before, and he went up for a day to show the local carpenter how to install the glass," says Peter. "And the cost was lower than cedar siding. Lacking that expertise, it wouldn't have been affordable."

Sustainability was another factor that shaped the design. There's a lot of clear

glass, but it's a weekend house and doesn't need to be heated or cooled through the week. To conserve energy, all the wet rooms are stacked in an insulated central core with small openings, so that only a quarter of the 230 sqm interior needs to be heated while the house is empty. Bedrooms and the living areas face north, with plenty of clear glass to enjoy views of the distant Catskill Mountains.

The staircase is painted yellow, and is south-facing to absorb the heat of the sun. In winter, it acts as a heat sink to warm the house; in summer, the accumulated hot air can be swiftly vented, drawing in cool air from the north side and eliminating the need for air conditioning.

In many parts of the world, proposing a glass tower in a region of great natural beauty would have encountered stiff

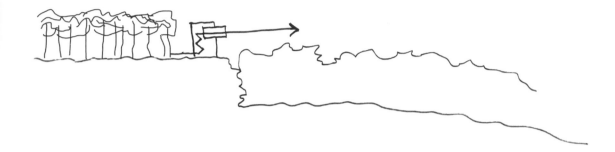

The living areas are cantilevered from a tower containing the bedrooms and a staircase that acts as a thermal chimney, warming the house in winter and drawing in cool air in summer. Glass curtain walls command sweeping views and dissolve into reflections of the trees (see page 144).

resistance, but this is a small rural community in which most buildings are out of sight of their neighbours. It's a place where the zoning department is open for only two hours every Wednesday morning and the chief of the fire department is a local pig farmer.

Within, the house is divided into three zones: the stack of bedrooms, each with its own bathroom; the open-plan living area; and the roof terrace, which commands a 360-degree view over the tree canopy. The floors are white-painted wood to disengage you from the ground, and the glass never needs cleaning because of the sheer surface and absence of pollution. At night, the house glows like a beacon,

and LEDs on the cable rail of the darkened staircase resemble fireflies in the forest.

The Glucks planned the house as a laboratory in which to test ideas of materiality and structure. "To save costs, we used a lot of wood framing in addition to the steel," says Thomas. "There were all kinds of crazy experiments; as builders, we understand that stuff. But what I treasure the most—even if it's just for a few hours—is the response from friends of my young son and daughter, and of people who know nothing about architecture. They feel it. We trusted our instincts and the result far surpasses our expectations."

# ROBERT KONIECZNY

# THE ARK

# BRENNA, POLAND

From a distance, it does look as though an ark has made landfall on a green hillside surrounded by farms. Fully shuttered, the house is an enigmatic object, a minimalist sculpture that seems to hover and rotate above the ground. The blank walls, pitched roof, and recessed base appear as a concrete monolith. Sheep use it as a scratching post, and horses have trampled the up-lights set into the ground, although they haven't yet tried to enter, two by two.

Robert Konieczny, who heads KWK Promes in Katowice, remembered childhood camping trips to the rolling hills of southern Poland and went looking for a site where he could build a weekend and summer house for his wife, Patrycja, and their daughter. By good fortune, a farmer was willing to sell a 2,000 sq m plot in the middle of a large, sloping field. Konieczny has designed forty innovative houses, of which ten have been realized, and he took his time to develop an ambitious project for himself. Two years

passed before he could begin construction, for landslides are common in this area, and the authorities were reluctant to allow him to build on an unstable hillside.

By the time a permit was granted, the architect had grown concerned and asked an engineer what he should do to avert slides. "Sit on the land as lightly as possible," was the response. "If you cut deeply, the water has a barrier to build up against." Konieczny realized that the

solution was not to challenge nature but to go with the flow, which dictated a different design. That was unwelcome news to his wife, however, who complained that she had waited too long for the first concept and didn't want more years to elapse before there was another.

"I'll do it in three days," Konieczny promised her, for he had been thinking about a house of his own for a decade. A tight deadline would concentrate his mind and

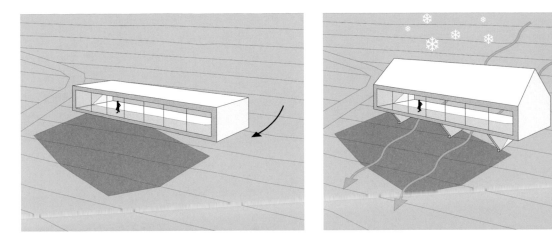

The Ark is rotated off
the slope and supported
on three concrete wedges
to minimize the foundations
and allow snow melt
to flow freely underneath.

Walls of polished stainless steel make the compact suite of bedrooms and bathrooms appear much larger.

# DRAWING ON THE PAST

In every age, architects have been inspired by past achievements. Leon Battista Alberti (1404–1472) interpreted the rules of Vitruvius for the builders of the Renaissance. Andrea Palladio (1508–1580) drew on his study of classical ruins to create villas that were emulated by English landowners two centuries later. Thomas Jefferson (1743–1826), the gentleman-farmer turned statesman, immersed himself in history and theory before creating his trio of masterpieces: Monticello in Charlottesville, Virginia; the "academical village" of the University of Virginia; and the Virginia State Capitol, a Roman temple for the new republic. His taste and erudition made up for a lack of architectural training, and Monticello was the still center of a peripatetic life, a place from which he could survey and manage his domain.

Thomas Jefferson spent forty years building and tweaking Monticello as a testing ground for his ideas on living.

From 1769 to 1809, Monticello was a work in progress. "Architecture is my delight, and putting up and pulling down one of my favorite amusements," Jefferson declared. His house was a testing ground for ideas derived from Palladio and the buildings he saw in Paris as the second US minister to France, and his invention shows in every part of it, from the interplay of geometric forms to the bed set in an alcove and the ingenious labor-saving devices. Everything was freshly thought-out. Now that Monticello has become a revered national shrine, it's hard to appreciate how radical a departure it was from the sober Georgian mansions of Jefferson's contemporaries.

Another architectural self-portrait, which continues to surprise and delight, is the trio of houses that Sir John Soane (1753–1837) built or remodeled for himself in London. A near-contemporary of Jefferson,

Soane went on the Grand Tour and became an architect of such originality that he was able to complete only a few buildings; even fewer have survived intact. He was an obsessive collector, and the houses (now a beloved museum) contain a magpie hoard of architectural fragments, sculpture, paintings, and books crammed into a three-dimensional labyrinth. More interesting to his fellow architects are the two breakfast rooms, with their shallow arches and flattened domes—devices for expanding cramped spaces that he adapted to grander houses like Wimpole Hall in Cambridgeshire. Soane's playful take on classical models and the brilliance of his inventions were long in eclipse, but have become a major source of inspiration since the 1970s.

Sir John Soane combined three terrace houses in London to display his varied collections and demonstrate his inventiveness.

Charles Moore (1925–1993) was a sponge, soaking up impressions as he traveled the world, and shedding the surplus as a charismatic teacher and prolific architect and writer. He built or remodeled eight houses for himself, as his practices and academic posts moved from Berkeley to Yale, UCLA, and the University of Texas. Each is a treasury of witty references, and the condominium at Sea Ranch on the California coast has achieved iconic status.

Moore's ranch house in Austin, Texas, is almost as crowded with collections as Soane's house-museum, and he was as restless an inventor as Jefferson. "Houses have given me the freedom to try new ideas," he declared. "If I don't like what I've done, I move on."

In *The Place of Houses*, a book co-authored with Gerald Allen and Donlyn Lyndon and first published in 1974, Moore wrote: "A house is in delicate balance with its surroundings and they with it. A good house is a created thing made of many parts economically. It speaks not just of the materials from which it is made, but of the intangible rhythms, spirits, and dreams of people's lives. Its site is only a tiny piece of the real world, yet this place is made to seem like an entire world. In its parts it accommodates important human activities, yet in sum it expresses an attitude toward life."

It would be hard to find a better definition of Taliesin, home to Frank Lloyd Wright (1867–1959) for the last five decades of his life. "Study nature, love nature, stay close to nature; it will never fail you," he told his apprentices. That the master heeded this advice in the house he built for himself near Spring Green in rural Wisconsin is clear to see. Begun in 1911, rebuilt after fires in 1914 and 1925, it is as much a part of the hillside as the rock outcrops and the mature trees that shade it. "Taliesin" means "shining brow" in Welsh—the language of Wright's mother's forebears—and refers to its placement below the crest of a hill. It remained the home Wright always yearned to come back to, and a showcase of his work that he constantly extended and reshaped.

Frank Lloyd Wright built Taliesin for himself near Spring Green, Wisconsin. It is as much a part of the hillside as the rock outcrops and the mature trees that shade it.

In contrast to Fallingwater, Taliesin has no one, iconic image. Its drama is muted, and demands a spirit of quiet contemplation. It emerges from dense foliage as a rambling, picturesque composition of limestone walls, sand-colored stucco balconies, and shingled roofs, and it reveals itself slowly, a little at a time. Within, every piece of art and furniture was strategically placed or grouped to guide one's view to the outside and heighten one's experience of the interior. In 1932, Wright established the Taliesin Fellowship, a school of architecture that continues to flourish, both here and in its winter home of Taliesin West in Arizona.

Rudolph Schindler (1887–1953) moved from his native Vienna to Chicago to work for Wright. In 1920, he relocated to Los Angeles to supervise construction of the Hollyhock House before launching his own practice. The house-studio he built for himself and his bohemian wife, Pauline, in 1922 is still one of the most daring experiments in living ever constructed. Tilt-up concrete panels separated by narrow glass strips support a flat redwood roof, and wood-framed glass sliders open onto outdoor rooms defined by hedges. As Schindler explained, each person would receive a large private studio, each couple a shared entrance hall, bath, and enclosed patio with an outdoor fireplace. There were open roof porches for sleeping and a shared kitchen. A tall screen of bamboo fences the house off from the traffic and the apartment buildings surrounding the empty field that Schindler found in what is now West Hollywood.

Rudolph Schindler launched his practice with a radical house-studio in West Hollywood, giving two couples personal and shared live–work spaces.

The concept of a cave with a canvas screen across the opening was inspired by a camping trip to Yosemite, and Schindler naïvely supposed that one could live and sleep outdoors year-round in Southern California. The concept of outdoor living rooms, warmed by open hearths, was a seductive idea, but winter rains, spring fogs, and chilly nights drove the residents indoors, as did the experience of trying to sleep on the roof. Although the utopian plan provoked endless tensions, between the Schindlers (who formally separated, communicating by pushing notes under each other's door) and a constant stream of artistic tenants, it fulfilled its maker's vision. The house cast a spell and shaped lives; it is full of passion and promise for Schindler's later work.

Konstantin Melnikov (1890–1974) was a "solo architect in a mass society," as his biographer, S. Frederick Starr, described him. He was deeply committed to the Soviet Union, choosing to return there following a *succès d'estime* in Paris, where he had designed the Soviet Pavilion for the 1925 Exposition des Arts Décoratifs and proposed a garage that would have spanned the Seine. Buoyed by commissions for workers' clubs, he leased a plot of land at the heart of Moscow and, in 1929, built himself one of the few private houses to be realized in that era of collectivization.

Inspired by grain silos and the rounded side chapels of Orthodox churches, Melnikov developed the concept of cylindrical forms, which he had been sketching since 1918 and incorporated into several of his public buildings. The house comprises two interlocking cylinders: a taller one pierced with 128 hexagonal windows, and a shorter one with a south-facing roof terrace, a flat glazed facade, and an embossed inscription of his name and profession in Cyrillic capitals. He played with variations on traditional building practices, using egg-crate wood floors and load-bearing brick walls that were coated inside and out with white plaster.

Melnikov may have seen his creation as a prototype for multiple housing, and it drew a stream of visitors and official delegations. Critics and rivals took it as a defiant assertion of individuality from an architect who had already been rejected by the feuding associations

One of the very few private houses in the former Soviet Union was built in Moscow by Konstantin Melnikov, a brilliant maverick whose career was tragically brief.

of his peers, and would soon be denounced as a formalist and denied official commissions. He continued to sketch and plead for rehabilitation, but would realize only one more building before his death at age eighty-four. It was a tragic loss to architecture, and the house—fought over by family members since the death of Melnikov's son in 2006—is teetering on the edge of ruin. But its very existence and survival are miraculous, and one can only hope that a private sponsor will make up for official neglect and fund a major restoration.

Eileen Gray (1878–1976), an Irish artist turned designer with a successful practice in Paris, fell in love with the rocky slopes of Roquebrune-Cap-Martin, overlooking the Mediterranean, and in 1926 bought a plot of land that had formerly been a lemon grove. Over the next three years, she designed and built a cubist white villa to share with her mentor, the Romanian architect Jean Badovici. She named it E-1027, code for her initials and his.

As a visionary designer and intuitive architect, Gray created a total work of art. Although modest in scale, E-1027 embodies the spirit of its era and the brilliance of a woman who has posthumously achieved the recognition she was long denied. There's wit in abundance, along with meticulous planning and a love of surprise.

Villa E-1027 was created by Eileen Gray on Roquebrune-Cap-Martin, high above the Mediterranean. It has recently been restored.

The house is aligned with the path of the sun, and louvered shutters open and tilt to provide shade and cross-ventilation. From the entrance, one can take different routes through the interior; an elliptical storage cabinet defines a foyer. Gray's bedroom adjoins the expansive living room, which opens onto the terrace through folding glass doors. Furniture, rugs, and colored tile floors demarcate zones for sitting, resting, washing, and working. Built-in storage units with pivoting drawers are an extension of the architecture. Lightweight tables of steel and glass can easily be moved onto the terrace, or adjusted in height. "External architecture," wrote Gray, "seems to have absorbed avant-garde architects at the expense of the interior, as if a house should be conceived for the pleasure of the eye more than for the well-being of its inhabitants. A house is not a machine to live in... Not only its visual harmony but its entire organization; all the terms of the work combine to render it human in the most profound sense." In later years, Gray observed that "the poverty of modern architecture stems from the atrophy of sensuality."

Le Corbusier offered generous praise for Gray's achievement after his first stay at the villa, but when he returned in 1938 as Badovici's guest, he declared that he had "a furious desire to dirty the walls." His eight lurid murals destroy the harmony of Gray's compositions. She was outraged and never returned. The murals were restored after wartime damage, acquired an importance of their own, and may have saved the house from demolition.

From his earliest years, Le Corbusier (1887–1965) was drawn to the Mediterranean, sketching ancient sites and vernacular buildings, and his vacations in the south of France strengthened this attachment. In 1952, the year he completed the Unité d'Habitation in Marseilles, he built Le Cabanon, a modest wood

Le Corbusier built Le Cabanon, a modest wood cabin with a meticulously planned interior, as a summer retreat on a site adjoining E-1027.

cabin on a tree-shaded spur of land adjoining E-1027. He called it a present to his wife, Yvonne, a native of Monte Carlo, and stayed there every summer until his death, swimming from the beach below.

Le Cabanon is a reinterpretation of the Primitive Hut, a concept devised by Marc-Antoine Laugier (1713–1769), and its simplicity may have been inspired by Le Corbusier's experience of lodging in monastic cells on Mount Athos, forty years earlier. From the outside, it appears as a log cabin with small window openings and a shed roof of corrugated fiber cement (in reality, the walls are composed of bark-covered pine planks that were precut in Corsica and shipped to the site). The interior, a 3.66 m square, is as meticulously planned as E-1027, but on a much smaller scale. The floorboards are painted yellow, the ceiling comprises panels of different colors, and the walls are raw plywood. Although seemingly artless, every detail has been precisely calculated. Inward-opening shutters are lined with mirrored glass to expand a view and pull in more light; paintings are as fully integrated as the marquetry table, shelf-units, and bed. It's intended as a retreat and for slumber. The owner would bathe outside in the shade of a carob tree, use a simple shed as his studio, and have his meals next door at L'Étoile de Mer, a casual restaurant owned by his friend Robert Rebutato, for whom he built a block of five holiday cabins on the slope above.

Eliel Saarinen (1873–1950) joined his two young partners in 1902 to build Hvitträsk, a house outside Helsinki in which they would live and work. It was an expression of the romantic nationalism that asserted the Finns' independence from their Russian masters, and it launched Saarinen on a successful career. After coming second in the 1922 competition to design a new headquarters for the *Chicago Tribune*, he decided to stay on in the booming American Midwest. He was appointed master planner and director of the Cranbrook Academy of Art, a complex located in a leafy suburb of Detroit. There, in 1930, Saarinen built a spacious home for himself, his wife, Loja, and their son, Eero.

The house's red-brick facade, tiled roof, and leaded windows, as well as the walled sculpture court at its rear, all recall the domestic architecture of William Morris, the English champion of arts and crafts. The interior is much more progressive. On the ground floor, open, light-filled volumes flow one into another: a spacious foyer, library, living room, and studio. Only the octagonal dining room, with

its softly glowing fir paneling, Chinese red niches, and shallow gilded dome, suggest a Scandinavian country house of the early nineteenth century. Saarinen's desk occupies one of the raised alcoves at either end of the long, barrel-vaulted studio, which doubled as a reception area. The owners' personal tastes are best revealed in the private rooms upstairs. The master bedroom was furnished eclectically, and the spacious master bathroom, with its expanses of plain tile and Vitrolite and its functional ceiling lights, evokes the Bauhaus.

Richard Neutra (1892–1970) made his debut in Berlin, designing four small houses as an assistant to Erich Mendelsohn. In 1925, Neutra emigrated to the US, briefly worked for Frank Lloyd Wright at Taliesin, and then moved to Los Angeles, sharing the house of Rudolph Schindler, with whom he formed a short-lived partnership. The steel-framed Lovell Health House, dramatically cantilevered from a hillside, brought him fame, and he was invited to lecture in Europe. A Dutch industrialist, Cees van der Leeuw, recognized his talent and offered to finance a residence that Neutra would build for himself and his family. The VDL Research House in LA was completed in 1932 on a site bordering the Silver Lake Reservoir. As the name suggests, it was a tribute to its enlightened sponsor and a place to test innovative materials and concepts of living. The two-story, 214 sq m house used conventional wood-frame construction, clad with white stucco, and silver-painted mullions supporting a ribbon of steel-framed windows—a formula that Neutra would employ throughout his forty-year practice. Trees shaded the west side.

Never was an architect's house put to better use. Neutra's drafting room and private office shared the ground floor with bedrooms for guests and one or two of his three sons; the upper floor contained open living areas and two bedrooms opening onto an outdoor sleeping terrace. A ladder led up to a roof terrace overlooking the reservoir. Life and work were intertwined: Neutra would often make sketches upstairs and send them down in a lift to be developed by his assistants; in the early years, these included Gregory Ain, Harwell Hamilton Harris, and Raphael Soriano. New materials were donated by manufacturers, and the house was used as the backdrop to an Oldsmobile advertisement under the tag line, "Modern to the Minute!" Neutra added a guest house to the rear, mostly used by his growing sons.

In 1963, the main house was destroyed by fire, and was rebuilt on the original footprint under the supervision of Neutra's son Dion. A rooftop reflecting pool was added, along with new materials and tall aluminum louvers to shade windows exposed by the loss of mature trees. The office was relocated and replaced by a seminar room and a music salon for Neutra's wife, Dione, an accomplished cellist. Shortly after Neutra's death in 1970, she wrote, "With the many glass surfaces, mirrors, pools that reflect trees and flowers, every step from room to room, stairway up and down, is an aesthetic and artistic experience."

Walter Gropius (1883–1969) founded the Bauhaus in 1919, fled Hitler's Germany to take up a teaching post at Harvard in 1937, and shaped the thinking of a whole generation of architects. As an immigrant, he wanted to settle down with his wife and daughter in a house that was conveniently close to his office in Cambridge, Massachusetts. It would be furnished with the sleek furniture he had retrieved from his apartment in Berlin, but had to fit in with its neighbors. The taut skin of vertical clapboards rising from a fieldstone base, the screen porch and the fences that extend from either side, as well as the central stair hall with rooms opening off on two levels, are features that Gropius admired in local farmhouses.

Visitors can enjoy the property on two levels: as a daring experiment, crammed with fresh ideas and novel artifacts, and as an enduring part of New England heritage. Early settlers adapted European models to the local climate and building materials; Gropius did the same, rooting modernism in this stony soil, and impressing skeptical neighbors when his house survived the great hurricane of 1938.

Bauhaus founder Walter Gropius, who became head of the Harvard Graduate School of Design in 1937, abstracted the New England farmhouse in Lincoln, Massachusetts.

The clean lines and functional furnishings are enlivened with personal touches, from the sinuous, hand-welded steel stair rail to the glass wall between bedroom and dressing area that allowed the owners to sleep with open windows while conserving heat in the rest of the house. Gropius's adopted daughter, Ati, loved the fact that her bedroom opened onto a roof deck and an outside spiral staircase that allowed her to come and go as she pleased. In this frugal, compact, energy-efficient house, Gropius showed Americans how they might live, simply and in close touch with nature—as Henry David Thoreau had, for his contemporaries, almost a century before.

When Luis Barragán (1902–1988) was awarded the 1980 Pritzker Architecture Prize, he declared, "My architecture is autobiographical." Indeed, with its elemental minimalism, Barragán's later work drew directly on his interest in the legacy of colonialism, European rationalism, and the polychromatic simplicity of provincial Mexican villages. In accepting the award, Barragán spoke of the qualities he cherished the most, including religion and myth, beauty, solitude, serenity, and joy. His house in the Tacubaya district of Mexico City, completed in 1948, is the first of his buildings to embody all of these virtues. The facade is plain, the plan unremarkable, but visitors are caught up in the intangible magic of the spaces in which the architect spent the last forty years of his life, often in seclusion.

Spare and solidly built, the house has a timeless harmony of the kind Barragán found in old churches, or in his gardens and fountains. All the elements play off one another, from the vibrantly colored rough stucco walls to the unrailed flights of stairs—basalt leading up from the hall, and cantilevered wood treads hugging

In Mexico City, Luis Barragán's house has a timeless simplicity, enriched by his love of color and earthy materials.

a wall of the studio. The lofty living room is lit by a wall of glass, set into the masonry and supported by a cross that divides the green wilderness beyond into a quartet of vistas. A walled roof terrace, paved with rough tiles, immerses you in a field of colored planes that frame the sky. Simple wooden furniture and a few paintings by Barragán's favorite artists—including a gold-painted canvas by Mathias Goeritz—are strategically deployed. It's a total work of art, masterfully understated, and as subtle a blend of ingredients as a Oaxacan mole sauce.

Philip Johnson described his Glass House in New Canaan, Connecticut, as a steel cage with a glass skin slipped over a brick chimney.

When Frank Lloyd Wright came to see Philip Johnson (1906–2005) in his newly completed Glass House, he stepped inside, looked around, and asked mockingly: "Am I indoors or am I out? Do I leave my hat on or do I take it off?" The host was delighted, for the spirit of creative play is alive in this house, as well as in the dozen other structures that joined it on a 16 hectare estate that was once a farm and retains its drystone walls.

Johnson was the chameleon of twentieth-century architecture. After launching his career as a fervent advocate of modernism, he briefly practiced what he preached before switching allegiance to a dizzying succession of styles. The Glass House belongs to the period in which he venerated Mies van der Rohe, collaborated with him on the design of the Seagram Building in New York, but found ways of distinguishing his own work from that of the master. Completed in 1949, it was Johnson's first major building, and it seems low-key and down-to-earth compared to the aloof temple of Mies's Farnsworth House. "I was building an American house," Johnson explained. "I like to get outdoors quickly, so I raised it only two steps above the ground. It's anchored by a brick podium and a brick cylinder that penetrates the roof. Mies didn't like that. His philosophy was based on uninterrupted floating planes." The cylindrical brick bathroom and fireplace was inspired by a wartime memory of a wooden village that had burned down, leaving only the masonry elements standing. "Over my chimney I slipped a steel cage with a glass skin," he said.

There is a pleasing informality to the way one enters through a sliding glass door—often followed by dry leaves, which blow in and settle on the herringbone brick floor. Mies furniture is placed in sculptural groupings to define the dining and sitting areas; the bed is concealed by an armoire. "It's often written about as a house you cannot live in," Johnson told me in the 1990s. "I don't know why—I've been going there for nearly forty-five years. Over the last ten, I've spent almost every weekend there, in all seasons— in fog, snow, and moonlight. It gets a little cold in winter, and warm in summer—but the doors give cross-ventilation. You adapt."

The house that Charles Eames (1907–1978) and the former Ray Kaiser (1912–1988) built for themselves in a meadow overlooking the Pacific occupies a similar footprint to the Glass House, and was completed a few months later. Charles, who practiced as an architect before becoming America's greatest twentieth-century designer, planned a single-story structure, cantilevered from a hillside. Published in the August 1945 issue of *Arts & Architecture* magazine, it was one of the first of the postwar Case Study Houses sponsored by the magazine's editor, John Entenza. It was to be built entirely of standard elements, ordered from catalogues. In late 1948, after steel had been delivered to the site, Charles changed the plans. Acting on his conviction that "design depends largely on constraints and the designer's enthusiasm for working within them," he sketched a two-story house and a separate studio, thus enclosing much more space while using the same structural elements, plus one extra beam. Red, blue, black, and white stucco panels, together with a grid of slender columns and glazing bars, turn the exterior into a three-dimensional Mondrian, screened by eucalyptus trees.

Charles and Ray Eames in the ICONIC house they built on a meadow overlooking the Pacific, enlivening the interior with color and pattern.

Within the 140 sqm house, a sleeping gallery with sliding screens overlooks a nearly cubic living room; tucked in below are a seating nook and a kitchen/dining area. Ray, who trained as an artist, collaborated on the design and furnished the space with a mixture of Eames furniture, folk art, plants, and found objects, infusing the clean-lined shell with color and pattern. Although she would have bristled if anyone had called her an interior designer, she made this sharp-edged container a sensuous live–work space. The house is maintained by Charles's grandson, Eames Demetrios, and is being meticulously restored with assistance from the Getty Conservation Institute.

Lina Bo Bardi (1914–1992) was an idealistic Italian architecture graduate when she and her new husband, a journalist turned art dealer, emigrated to Brazil in 1946 and settled in São Paulo. There, she struggled to realize her vision, starting with the house she completed in 1952. The Casa de Vidro is located in Morumbi, a planned community in the hills of a former tea plantation that is now part of the sprawling metropolis. Her's was the first residence in the neighborhood, and was intended as a model for those to come. The main house is as dramatic as the Eameses' original scheme: a single-story glass pavilion with a hollow-slab concrete floor and folded roof raised on ten slender steel posts. A light well accommodates an existing tree, while other trees have swallowed up the glass pavilion (providing much-needed shade) and the stone-built service wing to the rear. Visitors could park their cars under the house and enter it by a staircase that leads up from below.

Lina Bo Bardi's Casa de Vidro in São Paulo comprises a glass-walled living room, elevated on slender steel poles, with a service block to the rear.

There's a sharp contrast between open social areas and tightly enclosed private spaces. Within the luminous shell, and particularly in the 19 m long living room, Bo Bardi defined distinct zones using groups of furniture, including several items of her own design. An eclectic mix of pieces—old and new, Brazilian and European— is deployed on the blue mosaic floors, making this a congenial meeting place for the artists and architects the couple befriended. Although Bo Bardi was able to realize only fourteen of her many designs before her death, Casa de Vidro is a memorial to a rare talent that, like Eileen Gray, has achieved posthumous recognition.

Oscar Niemeyer (1907–2012) was proud of his membership of the Brazilian Communist Party, going into exile during the military dictatorship of 1964–85, but he never let that commitment interfere with his love of life and the curves of a woman's body, which he sketched joyfully and translated into architecture. He created some of the first great monuments of Brazilian modernism, from the Ministry of Education in Rio de Janeiro to the new capital of Brasilia. Midway through that dizzying ascent, Niemeyer built a second house for himself in the forested hills above Rio. The Casa das Canoas, completed in 1953, was a self-portrait of this architect-hedonist—as much a symbol of a carefree bachelor as the then contemporary Jaguar XK 120.

In the hills above Rio de Janeiro, Oscar Niemeyer built his curvilinear Casa das Canoas as a hedonistic self-portrait, responding to the topography of the site.

As Niemeyer explained to art critic David Underwood, "My concern was to design this residence with complete liberty, adapting it to the irregularities of the terrain, without changing it, and making it curved, so as to permit the vegetation to penetrate, without being separated by the straight line. And I created for the living rooms a zone of shade so that the glazed walls wouldn't need curtains and the house would be transparent as I preferred."

Descending a ramp to the house, one sees a sinuous plane of concrete hovering over a curved expanse of glass. A granite boulder emerges from an elliptical pool and trees tower high overhead. Beyond, where the ground drops away, bedrooms are tucked under the main floor and a terrace looking out to the ocean. Polished granite pavers in the open-plan living area flow out beneath the room-height glazing and slender steel mullions, blurring the boundary between indoors and out. There's a mix of modern Brazilian and European furniture, including the Thonet bentwood armchair that Le Corbusier favored. A curved screen wall veneered with richly grained peroba-do-campo wood embraces a circular dining table in homage to Mies's Villa Tugendhat. For all these nods to his mentors, Niemeyer's house is unmistakably Brazilian; indeed, in her scholarly study of the architect, Styliane Philippou likens its multiple rhythms to those of a samba.

Jean Prouvé (1901–1984) had no formal training, besides his apprenticeship to metalworkers in his native city of Nancy, but became one of the most influential designer-artisans of the twentieth century. Functionalism was his guiding principle. The prefabricated steel and aluminum buildings that were erected in postwar France and shipped to its African colonies were way ahead of their time, and his furniture, fabricated inexpensively for public institutions, is now eagerly collected as shabby-chic trophies by leaders of fashion. "It's important to take Prouvé away from the decorators and give him back to architects," says Robert Rubin, who funded the rescue and restoration of three tropical houses from war-torn Brazzaville.

Forced to leave his workshops in Nancy, Jean Prouvé and his family assembled a frugal house from aluminum panels originally intended for a prefabricated school.

Few of Prouvé's peers appreciated his genius during his lifetime, and in 1952 he was compelled to leave the workshops he had established to manufacture his designs. That prompted him to create a low-budget house for his family on a steep hillside in Nancy, using plans drawn by his younger brother, Henri. Prouvé had earlier worked for Air France, scavenging war surplus; now, he used his US army jeep to carry off aluminium panels (with his trademark portholes) that had been made for a school but were never used. The Maison du Coteau incorporated other fragments of factory production, and the whole family pitched in to build it in the summer of 1954.

As in all his buildings, Prouvé made a virtue of frugality. The linear plan comprises three compact bedrooms and a bathroom to the left of the entrance; to the right is an open-plan living/dining area that extends forward and is fully glazed on two sides. End walls are concrete, ceilings and partitions are plywood—inexpensive materials that are nonetheless thoughtfully detailed. The inner wall of the living room is filled with bookshelves and cabinets designed by Charlotte Perriand for the Cité Universitaire in Paris; the rest of the furniture is by Prouvé, except for a table gifted by Pierre Jeanneret. Soon after Prouvé's death, the city bought the house from his widow and currently leases it to a sympathetic tenant to ensure that it remains a living entity, while doubling as a house-museum.

Ulrich Franzen (1921–2012) was an unabashed modernist. After studying under Walter Gropius and Marcel Breuer at Harvard, he worked with I. M. Pei before launching his own practice with the house he designed for his family in Westchester County, New York. Completed in 1956, it was included in *Architectural Record*'s first annual round-up of the houses of the year, and it appears as fresh and viable today as when it was new. In a break with tradition, the magazine photographed the house with the couple, their three small children, and large Dalmation enjoying their daily routines.

The freestanding roof frame—two elongated diamonds supported on eight slender columns—was erected in a day. Its bold profile anticipates that of Le Corbusier's Heidi Weber house in Zurich; it also evokes the slender bow ties favored by architects of the era. The symmetrical plan is Franzen's homage to Mies: five low brick walls that seem to slide past the raised and covered terraces at either end and the glass-walled living area. Behind the wide hearth are two bathrooms and four bedrooms backed up to a solid rear wall. The wood-paneled ceiling echoes the slopes of the roof frame. Folding screens fanned out from the glass to display artworks, and the light-filled spaces were furnished with an anthology of modern classics, from Breuer to Gio Ponti and Florence Knoll.

Ulrich Franzen launched his career with a house for his family in Rye, New York, employing a prefabricated steel roof frame supported on eight slender columns.

Few architects have made such an assured debut, and none of the sixty houses Franzen would design over the next forty years would have quite the same iconic simplicity. Gropius wrote to praise "a bold, visual triumph over the gravity of inanimate materials," and the house is now enjoying a second life. Fernando Barnuevo, a Spanish aficionado of modernism, rescued it from demolition, and restored it with the advice of Franzen himself, who was living in retirement near Santa Fe. In 2007, Barnuevo moved in with his wife, Gloria, and their five children. "The house has changed our lives," says Gloria. "It's like a stage that has to be shared with others, and it has brought us much closer together. We can glimpse deer and wild turkeys from our fireside, and stay in touch with every change in the seasons."

Albert Frey (1903–1998) was Le Corbusier's assistant on the Villa Savoye and Salvation Army hostel before moving to New York and co-designing Aluminaire, the prototype for a low-cost prefabricated house that survives intact on Long Island, although it never went into production. In 1934, Frey relocated to Palm Springs and spent the rest of his life there, designing a hundred buildings as the fledgling desert resort evolved into a city. He built two houses for himself, each a laboratory for innovative ideas. The first, begun in 1940 and twice extended, came to resemble a space station. In 1963, he moved into the San Jacinto Mountains—a reminder of his native Switzerland—and there, on a ledge of rock 65 m above the valley floor, built the house in which he would spend his remaining years.

A massive boulder anchors the light steel frame to the mountainside and serves as a room divider between the open living area and the compact bedroom at the east end. A corrugated metal roof with 20 cm of fiberglass insulation protects the interior from the fierce sun. It projects out to shade the walls of glass, which slide back to capture every breeze. A carport is tucked in beneath the pool terrace. The 110 sq m interior is as tightly planned as that of a yacht, with a galley kitchen and a dining-cum-drafting table overlooking built-in cabinets and sofa beds.

For his second house in Palm Springs, California, Albert Frey anchored a lightweight steel structure to a massive boulder on a mountainside above the city.

"I wanted something minimal that eliminated the inessential and required no maintenance," Frey told me when I visited him at the house just before his ninetieth birthday. He stayed young by rising at 5 a.m. in summer to swim and visit his job sites—something his former boss, a health fanatic, would have applauded. His buildings are equally timeless. "The job of an architect is to find the ideal structure and turn it into art," he declared. "Fashion has nothing to do with it."

Ray Kappe (1927–) is a master of interlocking spaces and carefully modulated light. A dedicated teacher who founded the Southern California Institute of Architecture (SCI-Arc), Kappe was a pioneer of sustainability and has designed some three hundred houses over a sixty-five-year career. Looking back at the fifty projects of his first decade, he recalls: "It was a very optimistic period. There were greater opportunities for young architects than there are today, and a spirit of collegiality. We built primarily for young couples, and we wanted everyone to enjoy the benefits of the modern house."

The residence that Kappe built for himself and his wife, Shelly, is often regarded as his masterpiece. Completed in 1967, it was shaped by its steep hillside site in Pacific Palisades, a mile to the north of the Eames House. After securing a permit and beginning construction, Kappe discovered that natural springs made it impracticable to build a conventional foundation, so he redesigned the house as a bridge of massive laminated beams spanning between and extending beyond six concrete towers set up to 12 m apart. The towers lofted a 370 sq m house at a 45 degree angle to the hillside, covering only 56 sq m of ground and sparing mature trees. They also served as skylit bathrooms, stairs, and studies—what Louis Kahn called "servant spaces."

Large rectangular concrete pads provide a series of steps up the hill from the street to the entrance, which is tucked in below the cantilevered living room deck. The music of the springs, moist vegetation, rough wood, and low portal all suggest a Japanese tea house, but on a heroic scale. One discovers the house a piece at a time, climbing finger-jointed steps from confined to soaring spaces. The steps ascend from the sunken studio to a sitting room looking over a living room, to the dining area, with an island kitchen and bedrooms at the upper level, leading out to the garden, from where a bridge leads back to the roof terrace. Eucalyptus trees shade the decks, and light from the clerestories at the sides balances that from the expansive windows at front and back.

Sir Michael Hopkins (1935–) and his wife and partner, Patricia (1942–), were newly married and studying at the Architectural Association in London when they bought a sixteenth-century house in Suffolk and spent the next ten years restoring it for themselves. The house-studio that launched their practice in 1976 was the polar opposite: a taut block of steel and glass that settled gracefully into a row of Regency houses in the London district of Hampstead. It was a declaration of principles and a test bed for the large commercial buildings they were planning. Michael, who had worked with Norman Foster, shared the latter's fascination with the lightweight, factory-made elements of the Eames House and Buckminster Fuller's Dymaxion House, but he and his wife's debut as fledging architects had its own distinctive character. Even now, with Hopkins Architecture a global practice whose achievements range from the Glyndebourne Opera House in Sussex to new high-rise cities, their house remains a signature work and their principal home.

Michael and Patty Hopkins deftly inserted their live–work capsule into a row of Regency houses in north London.

It is at once a time capsule for the short-lived enthusiasm around high-tech (a label that has outlived its relevance) and a timeless exercise in transparency and space. The Hopkins had only £20,000 to spend—incredible as that figure now sounds—and, like the Eameses, they made every penny count. The house had to occupy a tightly defined footprint of 10×12m, and because the site is 2.7m below the level of the street, it is entered from a footbridge at the upper level. Slender steel columns, spaced 2.1m apart, support a grid of lattice trusses. The roof deck, floors, and side walls are composed of profiled steel sheeting, the front and back of full-height sliding glass panels. The structural materials are fully exposed, except for the carpeted floors, and the interior space is divided up by prefabricated melamine-coated panels and venetian blinds. An industrial steel spiral staircase links the two floors.

One would expect such a formula to be as utilitarian as a factory, but the opposite is true. The house has an elegance and precision that make it a good neighbor, and the sheer expanse of reflective glazing dissolves as night falls. Restrained color accents and metal-framed chairs by Mies and the Eameses animate the interior. The flexibility of the house has proved its worth, witnessing the growth of the architects' children and the relocation of their office.

Frank Gehry (1929–) had to fight for respect and commissions in his adopted city of Los Angeles. Before the Walt Disney Concert Hall, before his use of 3D modeling software and the prestigious commissions around the world, Gehry called himself a cheapskate

Frank Gehry wrapped a humble Dutch colonial house in a carapace of wood, corrugated metal, and chain-link fencing, creating a Los Angeles icon.

architect, taking his inspiration from adventurous artists. The "dumb little house" he remodeled for his family in 1978, using raw plywood, chain-link fencing, and corrugated metal, confirmed his status as an outsider in LA, outraged his neighbors, and thrilled perceptive observers. As Philip Johnson observed, "His buildings are shocking... but they give you a mysterious sense of delight."

Forty years on, the house has been extended and partially obscured by plantings, but it remains an audacious work of art. Gehry wrapped a new house around the old, adding 74 sqm to the existing 195, to achieve "a tension between the two... and to layer space from the exterior to the darker interior." His goal was to capture the immediacy of a brushstroke on canvas and the unfinished character of a building under construction. The roughness of the materials, here and in other projects of that time, was an honest reflection of meager budgets. Gehry stripped stucco walls to the studs and removed the upstairs ceiling to reveal the roof structure. The kitchen/dining room was floored in asphalt, with an angled cube of wood and glass above, and became the center of activity. Light entered the house from every angle, and the entire composition felt as though it was in motion. Kenneth Frampton likened it to the collages of Kurt Schwitters.

The Silver Hut—vaulted aluminum pods bracketing a shaded interior courtyard— was Toyo Ito's response to the visual chaos of Tokyo.

The early work of Toyo Ito (1941–), who opened his studio in 1971, was a response to the visual chaos and ephemerality of Tokyo. Ito explored the concept of urban nomads inhabiting tent-like structures, and the Silver Hut, which he built for his family between 1982 and 1984, is an expression of that idea. Seven shallow, steel-framed vaults supported by concrete posts arch over an interior courtyard and the rooms that adjoin it on three sides. Trees shelter the house from public view, and so—as often happens in Japan—a unique building is swallowed up in a sea of tiled roofs and conventional facades.

The paved courtyard, which can be opened to the sky or covered with a retractable canopy, draws fresh air and light into every part of the house. The living/dining room runs along the north side, Ito and his wife's bedroom is contained in a half-buried concrete wing to the west with their daughter's room above, and a separate studio and tatami room extend out from the east side. By Japanese standards, it's expansive; Ito told me that his wife has used the courtyard for a catwalk fashion show. To Western eyes, it appears immaterial—like a marquee erected in the garden for a wedding reception. In fact, it's surprisingly resilient, and it anticipated the architect's use of lightweight vaults on much larger structures, such as the Yatsushiro Municipal Museum in Kumamoto prefecture. The house was Ito's passport to larger-scale projects, and it celebrates the feeling of lightness one experiences in all his work.

Mart van Schijndel created a house within the shell of a former warehouse in Utrecht, pulling in light and air from patios to either side.

Mart van Schijndel (1943–1999) won the prestigious Rietveld Award for the house he built for himself in historic Utrecht. Completed in 1992, it occupies the shell of a former glazier's warehouse, and is concealed behind Van Schijndel's block of four revenue-generating apartments. Rigorous and inventive, the house achieves marvels within the straitjacket of the old walls. A triangular wedge of living space soars up to a two-story bar of bedrooms, bathroom, and kitchen at the wide end, stepping down to a workroom, study, and library at the other. Trapezoidal patios to either side pull in natural light through clear and translucent glass. Stucco end walls and ceilings are subtly colored: cool tones to intensify morning light, warm to enrich the glow of a sunny afternoon or compensate for gray skies. The outdoor–indoor divide is blurred in summer, and the patios make the living room feel much larger and more open.

Every detail of the interior was custom-made over a period of three years, in order to solve specific problems or test a new idea. Van Schijndel used his own inventive furnishings, alongside upholstered seating by Gerrit Rietveld, whose iconoclastic house for Truus Schröder-Schräder at the edge of Utrecht was a major source of inspiration. Glass doors swing open at the corners of the patios, and where the angle is acute, Van Schijndel has employed a double hinge on one door so that it can be shifted to one side to avoid a collision with the other. Bathroom and kitchen cabinet doors are hinged with silicon. A built-in chaise of perforated steel is tucked under a staircase, and thin aluminum panels are folded and attached to a wall to serve as bookshelves. Like Monticello, the house is a work of art and a demonstration of the owner's restless desire to experiment.

Inspired by the skeletal houses of Bali, David Hertz created a compound of sustainable wood and stucco blocks close to the ocean in Venice, California.

David Hertz (1960–) heads the Studio of Environmental Architecture in Santa Monica, California, and has been producing sustainable buildings since the start of his first practice in 1984. "I prefer being outdoors," says the avid surfer, "and when I think about being on the inside, I'm always considering how to pull in sunlight, fresh air, and views." The house he designed for his family in 1995 is located in Venice, a few blocks from the ocean, and was created to test his ideas on natural ventilation, energy generation, and recycled water, as well as the latest lighting technologies. But it doesn't shout about it. Rather, the house embodies a dream of sybaritic, open-air living.

Inspired by the skeletal wood houses of Bali, Hertz's design is a South Seas model adapted to the realities of Southern California, where a warm day is often followed by a chilly night, and security is an issue. The first phase comprised a pair of two-story volumes linked by a bridge; a decade later, the neighboring lot became available and the house was transformed into a compound of four blocks, all linked by bridges and wrapped around a lap pool. Sustainable woods, such as ipe, mahogany, and reclaimed fir, are employed throughout the house, while Hertz specified the use of his patented Syndecrete (which has half the weight and twice the compressive strength of regular concrete). That provides thermal mass to absorb the sun's heat, while rooftop solar collectors help generate 90 percent of the house's electrical needs.

The complex of house, studio, and guest house that Barton Myers built in a canyon to the north of LA is a mix of functional poetry and Palladian grandeur.

Barton Myers (1934–) built a 560 sq m live–work complex at the head of a secluded canyon in Montecito, 110 km to the northwest of Los Angeles. To preserve the beauty of the landscape, Myers (who shared the role of contractor with his wife, Victoria) put his studio at the top of the steep 16 hectare site, a guest house and garage below, and the main house on a level pad between. Lofty steel-framed pavilions have roll-up segmented glass doors that open onto terraces, and roll-down steel shutters to provide security when the owners are away, to protect the property from brush fires, and to screen the sun.

As an added safeguard, and to insulate the interiors from the heat of summer, each flat roof serves as a shallow pool, the water for which is taken from uphill storage tanks. Nature conditions the air, and a lap pool runs along the edge of the guest house roof. The complex, completed in 1999, was built inexpensively, and its boldly exposed, galvanized structures require little maintenance. The main house is as functional as a factory, but its grand proportions evoke classical temples and Palladian villas; it also puts a fresh spin on the California tradition of airy porticoes jutting forward from adobe masses.

Simplicity pays off in these stripped-down loft spaces. The great luxury is height, which brings uphill views and well-balanced light through clerestory windows in the studio and the living/dining area of the house. A cantilevered canopy over the south front of the latter shuts out the sun in summer, but allows it to warm the interior in winter. Master and guest bedrooms occupy low wings beside and behind the living area, and are separated by bathrooms and service spaces. These are linked by a corridor that runs behind double-sided book stacks.

With this house and the two that followed, Myers returned to a theme he had first explored fifty years earlier in Toronto, when he had built his family a contemporary steel and glass house on a site hemmed in by redbrick Victorians. "I thought—as so many modern architects have—that this singular house might serve as a prototype for high-density affordable housing." Sadly, that dream has yet to be realized.

Steven Ehrlich (1946–) lives on a quiet street in Venice, California, and the wall he wrapped around the corner site is a translucent membrane of white acrylic-fiberglass that catches the shadows of passers-by and glows from within at night. His two-story house, completed in 2005, exploits the linearity of the site, opening up on three sides through 5 m high glass sliders to a huge branching pine on the west side, an entry court/pool to the south, and a garden court to the east. There's a seamless link between indoors and out, concrete floor and hardscape. Outriggers over the pool support motorized red blinds that block the sun and provide another screen for the play of shadows. At the end of the site is a detached studio-guest house. The steel beams are exposed, and the three open sides are clad with rusted corten steel, backing up to a northern boundary wall of bead-blasted concrete block.

Muscular and raw, the house is softened by the presence of nature, the Donald Judd–like refinement of the gypsum plaster, and the Finn ply cabinetry. Ehrlich shares the house with his wife, journalist Nancy Griffin, and his three grown-up daughters sometimes stay the night in low-ceilinged pods suspended within the central void. There are other intimate hideaways, but the central stairs, art, and eclectic furnishings seem to float within an airy, light-filled volume. From every point, you are looking through and out, making this a minimal shelter with the maximum of emotional resonance.

"Venice is gritty and unpretentious and the house expresses that," says Ehrlich, who discovered the advantages of courtyard living during the six years he spent in Africa, including two as the Peace Corps' first architect in Marrakech, Morocco. "It's nice to be in a compound where you are open to the elements while enjoying privacy. Walk outside and you are part of a vibrant community."

Steven Ehrlich's ideas of living were shaped by his years as a Peace Corps volunteer in North Africa. His house in Venice opens to the elements.

# SCOTT JOHNSON

# WALL HOUSE

# OJAI, CALIFORNIA

Sleek high-rises are a specialty of the firm that Scott Johnson copartners, but the artistic side of his personality finds expression in houses. He tries to squeeze in one or two a year, and has designed four ground-up exemplars for his family. The latest is a weekend house of corten steel and glass, concrete and stone, a 90-minute drive north from the loft in downtown Los Angeles that he shares with his wife, Dr. Margaret Bates.

"We started looking for a site in Malibu because I love the enormity of the ocean," says Johnson. "Meg prefers the forest, and I realized we'd never have the privacy we wanted on the beachfront. Eventually, we found a linear, five hectare plot on the edge of a farm, which was flanked by creeks and two hundred oak trees to give it water and privacy. I grew up in Salinas Valley and my father was an agricultural researcher, so I know all about farmers. You don't negotiate the price. So I introduced myself to the owner, and shook hands on the figure he had given the agent. Best thing I ever did; I've had a blizzard of benefits in return.

"On the day I saw the site," Johnson continues, "I knew how the house should be oriented and where it was to sit. You learn through the making of houses what you're happy with and what you might do differently or go beyond. Here, I wanted a strong sense of a line on a flat site, with a public/solid wall on one side, and a private/transparent facade looking out to the trees on the other. I explored a number of iterations but it came together very quickly. Designing for yourself is a breeze after designing for others. Meg is a great client. She'll say a few things at the beginning and then let me go."

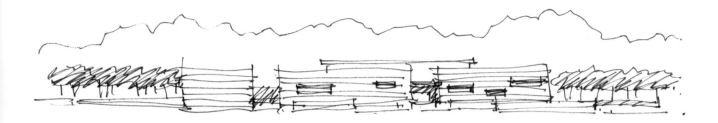

MASTER    STUDIO    LIVING/MUSIC    KITCHEN  BR.    OUTDR FP + KITCHEN    FOOD GARDEN

An earlier house high above St. Helena in Napa Valley comprised a series of boxes that responded to a steeply sloping site and sweeping views of forested mountains. The 560 sq m Wall House establishes its own sense of place on a *tabula rasa*. One drives up to a tall, impassive wall, 80 m long, which gives little hint of what lies beyond its narrow hooded windows and raised porch.

"It celebrates the ritual of arriving, penetrating the barrier, and immediately seeing the terrace and pool," Johnson explains. "It also has practical advantages—as a thermal wall to block heat gain from the westerly sun, as a solid surface for the display of artworks, and as psychological protection. As I get older, I value the

elemental. I want clarity, and I admire artists—including James Turrell, Walter de Maria, and Donald Judd—as much as I do architects."

Steel construction permitted long, unbroken spans and a feeling of openness. The house in St. Helena had a wood frame with a high degree of expansion and contraction—a living skin. Here, Johnson designed a plenum deep enough to contain a lateral truss, and suspended large panels of glass with silicon joints to form a sheer, column-free east facade. That experiment fed into a later project, the McCourt House in Beverly Hills, where a whole wall opens up like an accordion over 45 m. The Wall House is passively sustainable, with a solar array on the flat

To exploit a linear site, rooms
back up to a thermal wall
clad in corten steel, and
open through glass sliders
to a pool terrace and a vista
of trees and mountains.
Right, site plan showing the
ground floor. Key:

1   garden
2   bathroom
3   bedroom
4   kitchen
5   swimming pool
6   living room
7   entrance
8   media room
9   dance studio
10  art studio

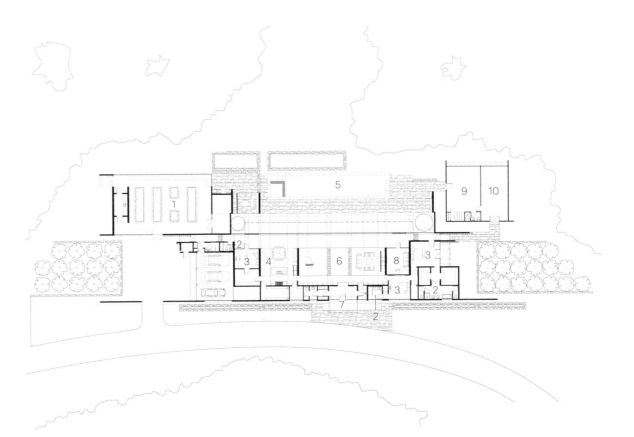

"As I get older, I value the elemental. I want clarity, and I admire artists—including James Turrell, Walter de Maria, and Donald Judd—as much as I do architects."

Scott Johnson

roof, radiant heating in the concrete floor, and a clerestory above the soffit to vent hot air. Gray water is stored in cisterns and used for irrigation. The corten facade is spaced out from the structural wall by Z-clips and thermal separators, and a deep canopy on the east side shades the glass in summer.

A binary plan, with the master suite at the south end, a guest bedroom to the north, and a long, open living space and kitchen in between, provides flexibility and wonderful exercise for the owners' feisty dog. Stone pavers root the house in the landscape, the board-formed concrete cross-walls and hearth catch the light, and a vine-clad pergola shades a dining patio. The living room is lined with books, and the

spare furnishings include several chairs designed by Johnson himself.

"We have a son who went to culinary school and want to tempt him back, so I consulted with him on the kitchen equipment," says Johnson. "And I have a daughter who sings with an accompanist so we gave the living room a drop ceiling that is pierced to create good acoustics, a raised dais, and a sunken seating area where we can entertain a crowd. Frequently, it's just Meg and me. She's in the garden or reviewing her clients' medical files; I'm in the garage painting—and will segue to the studio when it's built."

# JOSÉ SELGAS & LUCÍA CANO

# SILICON HOUSE

# MADRID

A sunken patio leads
to a glazed entry foyer,
with a living wing to the
left and sleeping areas
to the right.

Located on a 2,000 sq m wooded lot
in La Florida, on the outskirts of Madrid,
this house was shaped by a deep
respect for nature. The husband-and-
wife partnership of José Selgas and Lucía
Cano were close to buying a house in
the city center when they had their first
child and realized they needed a healthier
environment, with fresh air and the shade
of trees. "We were engaged in many other
projects at the time," recalls Selgas. "This
was just one more, and last on the list since
it was for us. We approached it as we
would for a client. Whenever we design a
house we think, what would it be like to sit
or sleep there? Can you afford this?"

The couple made a concept sketch of a
two-part house—a compact wing for living,
a long wing for sleeping—and moved it

around to preserve mature trees. That was
a challenge, because the gentle slope of
the site is covered with evergreen oak, elm,
ash, acacia, and plane trees, all seeded
by birds from surrounding properties. Each
tree was plotted on a site plan, and the
house (which has a fortuitous resemblance
to the shape of New Zealand) was inserted
between them. The single floor level is
half-buried in the slope to reduce its impact
on the landscape, and the excavated earth
was relocated to mounds that enrich the
natural topography of the lot.

The architects found another unencumbered
strip of land for their drafting studio:
a transparent tube of space that was
completed soon after the house, allowing
them to walk a few meters from home to
office. The site was officially categorized

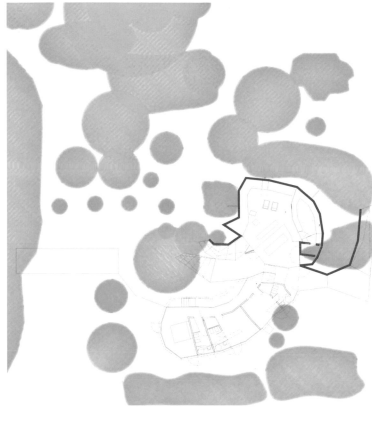

The house was shaped
and positioned to preserve
existing trees, as shown
in the site plan (above).

A ribbon window of acrylic is supported on low, poured-concrete walls. The house itself is sunk into the ground to minimize its impact on the land and enhance its sustainability.

as a swimming pool, and an inspector wondered why a second pool adjoined the house. "We love swimming," Selgas replied.

The couple, principals of SelgasCano, are masters of lightness and transparency and adore strong colors—as their 2015 Serpentine Pavilion demonstrated— and this 180 sq m house is a showcase of their design philosophy. It is also a laboratory in which to test ideas and materials. The architects conceived it as two unrailed viewing platforms, with the house tucked underneath.

The roof terrace edged with orange-painted steel shelters the living spaces; the blue-edged terrace is set lower and covers the sleeping areas. Steps provide easy access to both, and each helps to foster outdoor living, year-round, especially at sunset. The original plan was to cover the terraces with silicon tiles (hence the house's name). Instead, it was decided to use a 10 cm layer of rubber—scraps of

tires salvaged from about two hundred cars and mixed with resin—which provides good insulation and a springy surface to walk on. "Close relations with builders are critical—we can learn from them," says Selgas. "We are always involved with construction, even working as contractors ourselves. We did a lot of detailing on-site with the builder, but he abandoned the job just before finishing, saying, 'This is an experiment, not a house.'"

To enter, one steps down to a multilevel wood deck and the transparent link between the two halves. Acrylic is used in place of glass for the entry pavilion and the ribbon windows. It is colorless, reduces thermal gain and ultraviolet light, and is less expensive to bend. Low walls are poured concrete, and the formwork was recycled to provide the boards that clad the upper walls. Slender steel poles support the painted wood ceiling joists. The house opens up to the front and rear decks through acrylic folding doors. Orange

linoleum is employed in the kitchen, while other floors are painted concrete.

The open-plan living areas are frugal and playful. Three acrylic spheres pull light into the living room, and a ceiling vent allows hot air to escape. A steel hearth resembles a minimalist sculpture. Wall benches and storage are built in, a steel bookcase is suspended from the ceiling, and the movable furniture is lightweight and colorful. In the master bedroom, pulleys are used to raise and lower wooden shutters.

The house achieves a high level of sustainability through good insulation, the earth that cushions it, and cross-ventilation, with no need for air-conditioning. In fact, the climate in La Florida is cooler than in the city, where summer temperatures can stay at 40 degrees Celsius throughout the night.

"We love working with clients," says Selgas, "and our conversations with them always enrich our work. Here, where we were architects and clients, we missed those discussions. The main ideas came from Lucía, but our jobs are like palimpsests— the work of many heads and hands, adding, subtracting, and changing. The more people involved, the better for us."

# DON MURPHY

# SODAE HOUSE

# AMSTERDAM

Ivy-clad ruins inspired this sculptural house, whose rough surfaces welcome creeper and will eventually become as one with the land.

"When you design and build your own house," says Don Murphy, "it becomes a piece of you. People often say, 'Oh, it must be wonderful to be an architect and design your dream home,' and I respond, 'It's not a dream, it's a nightmare!' The more architecture, the more effort; everything that differs from the norm has to be taken care of. You need to create your own deadlines. With a client, making decisions in time and on budget is routine.

"My wife, Sylvie," he continues, "had seen magazine features on some of the five or six houses I'd done previously and urged me to do one for us. I said yes, but rather hoped I'd get off the hook." No chance: Sylvie, a fashion designer, found an extraordinary location beside the Amstel river on one of the oldest polders (drained land below sea level) in the Netherlands. The master plan developed for Amsterdam in the 1930s resembles a hand: the palm is the center, the fingers are the extensions of the city, and the spaces between are nature reserves—well-protected green wedges. Construction is limited to plots that have already been developed, so the Murphys bought a teardown in order to build their house.

The regulations prescribed a footprint of no more than 21×9m, wall heights, and two roofs with slopes of between 15 and 60 degrees. Murphy discovered that the owners of the land had hired another architect to design and secure approval to build a large thatched house. "I thought, my God, I couldn't live in something like that, but I knew that if we proposed something different we might not get permission," he says. "We sketched as many as fifty iterations before deciding on a linear concrete block with sloping walls and roofs. The municipal officials said, 'You can't do that,' but their lawyers found nothing in the rules that forbade sloping walls, and passed us on to the design review committee."

There was a public hearing, and Murphy won approval by explaining that traditional rural houses had small windows because farmers and fishermen were out in the open all day long, and when they returned home they wanted to be dry and comfortable. They weren't interested in gazing out onto the landscape, but professionals who spend their days in city offices look forward to doing just that. "We are trying to invent a new

typology for living in the country," says Murphy, "with a rough skin that welcomes plants and insects. A synergy with nature rather than a pristine contrast—like so many contemporary buildings that copy traditional styles but are glaringly white. Growing up in Ireland, I was intrigued by ivy-clad ruins. There are Second World War bunkers scattered around the Dutch landscape, and they become part of it. I wanted the house to be like that."

To maximize views over the landscape, Murphy put the living spaces on the upper floor with expansive windows, bedrooms underneath, and play areas in the basement (which had to be watertight, like an inside-out swimming pool). The top floor is at sea level; the cellar is 7m below. The structure combines a steel frame in three 7m bays with concrete blockwork, covered with insulation, metal mesh, and sprayed concrete that was troweled to give it sharp edges. The house opens up to water and meadows to the east, and is closed to the city-owned allotments on the west side. Sylvie was part of the design process, and

she and Murphy had long discussions about the amount of glass, a room for her dogs, and how radical the kitchen should be. They planned to call the house Soda for the family's initials: Sylvie, Oscar, Don, and Ava. Eden arrived as the house was being designed, so they added another letter.

The house achieves a high level of sustainability through its orientation, cross-ventilation, and abundant natural light. There's underfloor heating in the living areas and no need for air-conditioning, but Murphy admits that, if he were to start over, he would install a geothermal pump. "Every day we feel privileged to live here." he says. "Initially, some of the neighbors were annoyed with us. 'What an ugly house! How could you do something like this?' Now, when you drive by, you can hardly see it; it's half-covered with ivy. We've seen about eighty species of birds, including storks and herons, and even crayfish that come out onto the lawn. At night, we light candles outside to attract wildlife."

# ANDREA & LUCA PONSI

# CASA MAREMMA, MAGLIANO IN TOSCANA

# ITALY

Italians owe allegiance first and foremost to their home city and region; the country comes second (unless, of course, the national team is playing). Andrea Ponsi is deeply attached to Florence and his studio in Oltrarno, but he was born in the Tuscan port city of Viareggio, and that is where he began his quest to remodel a seaside house as a weekend retreat. Finding nothing he liked and could afford, he moved south along the coast and was able to purchase half a hectare of land in Maremma, an agricultural region of great natural beauty. The hilltop site surveys a rolling landscape of vineyards, olive trees, and farmhouses, with a view to Monte Argentario and the island of Giglio.

Building anything in Italy can be quite an ordeal, for construction is tightly regulated. In Maremma, no more new buildings will be approved away from existing settlements. Ponsi, however, was lucky: the former owner of the land he'd acquired had secured

a permit to build a traditional house for sale, and had already put in a drive and utility connections. The building department in the nearby town of Magliano approved the idea of a contemporary house within a very tight envelope, and made Ponsi an offer. If he would buy and demolish one of the ugly buildings they wanted to eliminate, he could add the footprint to his own house. That gave him an extra 35 sq m, while the building code allowed a little more for a garage, permitting him to enclose 200 sq m.

"This was a joint project with my son Luca, who is also an architect," says Ponsi. "We considered different designs, but the basic idea was clear: a house that echoes the horizontality of the landscape, gently descending to the horizon of the sea. It had to be simple and employ harmonious materials; it also had to be easy to maintain and secure when unoccupied." Ponsi and son devised a three-level structure in which the first floor is embedded in the hillside and exposed only on the entry facade,

Bands of tufo, white stucco, and dark boards serve to dematerialize the house, which seems to float amid the wooded hills of southern Tuscany (left). The living room opens onto a shaded pool terrace (opposite).

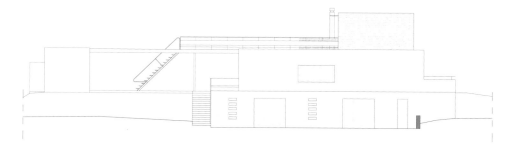

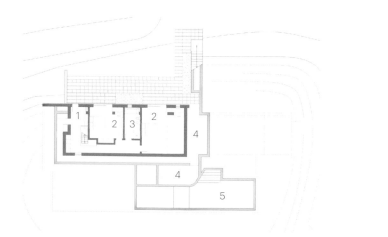

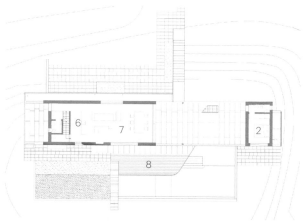

Eastern elevation (opposite, center) with plans of the ground and first floors (opposite, bottom, from left). Key:

1  entrance
2  bedroom
3  bathroom
4  plant room
5  swimming pool
6  kitchen
7  living/dining area
8  deck

where it is faced in tufo, a locally quarried volcanic rock, laid in alternating courses 10 and 15 cm deep. It contains two guest bedrooms (one of which stands in for the garage), houses mechanical services, and backs up to the pool. Steps lead up to a terrace, partially covered with a steel deck, which separates a linear living area from a third bedroom at the opposite end.

A pool floats off to the far side, leading the eye to the blur of the sea. This story is clad in white stucco and appears to float lightly above the ground. More steel steps lead up to the master suite, which is clad in dark boards. A concrete frame with insulated brick infill 30 cm deep provides good insulation and stability, but it's the skin that gives the house its character.

"I remember working for other offices in San Francisco, thirty years ago, and doing drawings that look a lot like this house," says Ponsi. "There's an image that has been there for years, which has fed into competitions and the house I did in Tiberon a decade ago. It grew with me, and finally I've realized it."

The design was approved, and Ponsi selected a local contractor, who did an exemplary job even though they had previously built only one modern house. Construction lasted about two years. The only hitch came early on, when Ponsi took a second look at a map of the site and realized that the dotted line he could see indicated a water main that would intersect the pool he was planning to extend out

"The landscape, the sky, and the house itself are a relaxing chamber. And every time I look I think, we could design a new chair, or add to the landscape."

Andrea Ponsi

from the house, rather than place at its side. "Happily, I wasn't on a schedule and could make changes," says Ponsi. "And I did the landscaping myself, learning as I went along. When I moved in, I wondered how we would irrigate the land. I spent a lot on a diviner who said there was no water; then, a few months later, my gardener recommended a new diviner, who charged only 50 euros and located a spring. We drilled 60 m down and now we have a well."

The house is sparely furnished with pieces designed by Ponsi himself, while the radiators and other fittings are in copper— long his signature material. Driving there in summer and whenever he can spare a weekend, the architect is reminded of the childhood holidays he spent with his grandfather in the mountains. It's a welcome escape from the heat and the tourist hordes invading Florence.

"The landscape, the sky, and the house itself are a relaxing chamber," says Ponsi. "And every time I look I think, we could design a new chair, or add to the landscape."

Architect-designed furnishings and fittings make extensive use of copper and wood (opposite). The upper-level master bedroom frames a distant sliver of the Tyrrhenian Sea (above).

A large holiday house for the architect and his extended family is split into two ground-hugging bars of concrete and glass that echo the line of the horizon.

his last stand in the military coup of 1973. In each of these projects, the goal was to fuse architecture and structure into a seamless whole; in the house, the projecting beams resemble a Donald Judd sculpture, playing off the rock-clad walls and the transparency of the glass balustrades and wraparound windows.

To achieve greater privacy from the narrow access road, public areas, and a neighboring property, the site was excavated around the two blocks, with the resulting mass of earth piled up behind retaining walls faced with locally quarried stone. This created a sunken enclosure for the pools

and landscaped courtyards, and reduced the impact of the blocks on the land. The hard surfaces are overgrown with climbing plants, which add color and a soft texture. "Length and magnitude were the guiding principles," explains Undurraga. "From afar, you see one line playing off the trees in the cemetery and the sculptural mass of the rocks, like a work of art extending from the horizon. As you approach, it becomes two strokes, and from the point of entry you see first one, then the other house end-on, where the scale is more domestic."

Although the enclosed space totals 924 sq m and includes ten bedrooms,

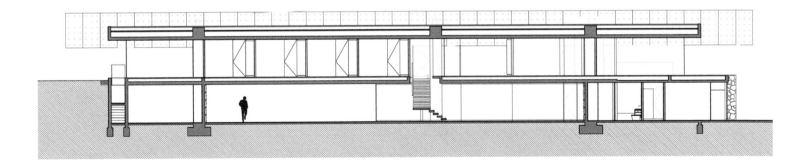

the house never feels like a hotel. The ground floor of each block is laid out like a dumbbell, with social spaces, kitchen, and children's playroom at either end, and an open space between to provide a shady terrace for summer dining and shelter from wind. This turns each bar of the dumbbell into a bridge. Glass sliders open onto the terraces and pool, providing cross-ventilation in summer and sweeping views. On clear days, one can glimpse the city of Valparaiso across the bay, 60 km to the south.

The corridors that serve the upstairs bedrooms face north, to be warmed by the sun in winter and shaded by louvered blinds in summer. Floors are of concrete, and are covered with ceramic tiles in the sleeping areas upstairs. Undurraga's wife,

Ana Luisa Devés, was his partner in the practice that bears their names but now divides her time between the family and her vocation as a sculptor. Her work is deployed around the house, complementing the spare modern furnishings.

The family assemble there as often as they can, and it's a lively place when children are frolicking in the pools and their parents are catching up on their scattered lives over leisurely lunches. But for Undurraga it can also be a retreat from the pressures of a city office, and there are plenty of places where he can seclude himself.

"To me," says the architect, "the house feels light rather than heavy, and it can be as quiet as a monastery. It's a great place to read, write, draw, and think about architecture."

# SUSANNE NOBIS

# HAUS IN BERG

# LAKE STARNBERG, GERMANY

"I thought it would be nice to raise my children in the country where they can see a cow, just as I did when I was young," says Susanne Nobis, explaining her decision to relocate from Munich to the shore of Lake Starnberg, a half-hour drive to the south. Her property is located in the idyllic Bavarian countryside at the foot of the Alps. It has long been a desirable place to live, and old mansions occupy the neighboring lots, opening off the tree-lined road that borders the lake. The cows have been relocated to pastures new, and the lake is thronged with weekend visitors, but the countryside retains its natural beauty and abundant wildlife.

Before moving to southern Germany, Nobis had lived in Berlin. She had also spent time in Genoa, camping out in the grand salon of a palazzo with mosaic floors, and hanging her clothes on a bamboo pole suspended from the ceiling. In Munich, she had rented a high-roofed space on the upper floor of a storage depot, living and working there for two years despite the lack of hot water and electricity. These experiences reinforced her preference for lofty, open volumes and an emphasis on basics.

The challenge was to design a house that would have a strong character of its own—something much smaller and quite different from its conservative neighbors—without exciting opposition. Inspiration came from the small boathouses on the lakefront: miniature barns with open ends that are often paired together. Those are made of wood; Nobis chose to clad her

design in ribbed aluminum to give the shell a crisp outline. Since this was to be both a family home and a workspace, it made sense to separate the different functions. Two rectangular pavilions of equal size sit side by side, one stepping forward a few meters of the other. Pitched roofs conform to the local vernacular, are quick to shed snow, and provide added height inside.

Nobis put the bedrooms over the studio in one pavilion, and the living spaces in the other, undivided volume, and linked them with a glazed entry foyer. The ends of both pavilions are fully glazed so that locals passing by can see straight through, and the floors are raised a meter off the ground on a recessed concrete base to provide a glimpse of the lake. Neighbors were initially apprehensive of this silvery apparition in their midst, but have come to accept it, all the more so as creeper has grown over a

climbing frame to either side and softened the outline. Lightweight steel steps, inside and out, strengthen one's impression that the house is floating above the ground.

To heighten the drama and increase efficiency, Nobis made the pavilions as long, high, and narrow as possible. Linear skylights in the pitch of the roofs pull in natural light and can be opened to vent hot air. Each pavilion points northeast, toward the lake, and opens onto a raised terrace overlooking a lawn to the rear. Hinged screens of aluminum tubes resembling gates can be manually operated to provide shade and privacy at both ends of the workspace, and at the southwest end of the living space.

The interiors are lined with knotty spruce, making them warm, tactile, and aromatic. Uplights intensify the sense of living within a well-crafted cabinet. That's a welcome sensation during the snowy winters, when the house glows from within and provides a snug refuge for work, relaxation, and entertaining. The living room is lined with built-in bookshelves, and the dining table is set on a raised platform. There's a strong emphasis on Bauhaus designs in the spare furnishings, a reminder that Germany was a cradle of modernism a century ago.

The simplicity of the forms is enriched by the different ceiling heights and the alternation of expansive and intimate volumes. The bedrooms have the feeling of an attic, with a narrow corridor linking the master bedroom overlooking the lake to a pair of bedrooms at the opposite end. These were made intentionally small to discourage the children from retreating to their private domains. The strategy worked, and the kids are now full-grown. "Living and working in the country, I don't feel cut off as much as when I had two babies who changed the pattern of my life," says Nobis. "I love the light, which changes every hour and moves around the floor and walls, casting shadows across the facades and the interior." She has designed six other houses, and the experience of living in the Haus in Berg (named for a nearby village) is sure to enrich her future work.

# REMO HALTER & THOMAS LUSSI

# TWIN HOUSES

# KASTANIENBAUM, LUCERNE

An enigmatic facade of dark concrete and shuttered verandahs conceals a three-level house to either side of a central wall, and a roof terrace accessed by a central staircase.

A block of black concrete, sharply cut away, rises from the woods that border Lake Lucerne. The entry is set back behind the carport, and a horizontal opening reveals nothing but unrailed flights of steps ascending to the roof. The grid of small round openings to either side is equally enigmatic. The building contrasts sharply with its more conventional neighbors in Kastanienbaum, an affluent suburb of Lucerne that is named for its chestnut trees. Remo Halter bought the site and designed a 520 sq m double house, allowing him to sell half of it and split the cost of the land.

Halter was then in partnership with Thomas Lussi, but now heads his own practice with his Brazilian wife, Cristina Casagrande. On work trips to her home city of São Paulo, Halter met the veteran architect Paulo Mendes da Rocha and spent time in his house—an experience that reinforced Halter's love of concrete as a building material, and of shadowy interiors that offer a tranquil retreat from busy lives. In his own house, it encouraged him to keep openings in the upper story to a minimum, while glazing the ground floor to pull in views of the woods. Black concrete absorbs the light, anthracite-lacquered cabinetry reflects it, and floors of Jatobá (a reddish Brazilian

cherry) add a rich glow. "The house was an experiment," recalls Halter. "My mother said, 'You are crazy; you want to live in a dark house? You need a psychiatrist?'"

Although Halter recently designed an all-white house in Brazil, he finds this one a good fit for himself and his wife, and an effective way of explaining his ideas on light and space to clients. It's a 10-minute drive from his office, but feels like a world away. Despite its sharp angles and hard surfaces, it has some of the character of traditional Japanese houses and their intimate relationship to nature. *In Praise of Shadows* (1933) is a favorite book of Halter's, and he takes a similar approach to that of its author, Junichiro Tanizaki: cherishing the contrasts between dark and light, and valuing every subtle transition from one to the other.

The vistas of trees and sky are intensified as one's eyes adjust to the expanse of green foliage. And the pools of darkness have a mysterious, even sensual quality. Happily, Halter found a congenial neighbor to live in the other half of the house—an elderly doctor who travels a lot, and shares his appreciation of a quiet retreat. They meet at the mailbox and occasionally have lunch together, but otherwise live separate lives.

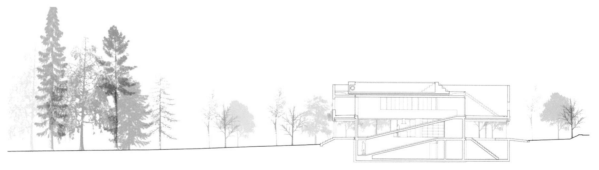

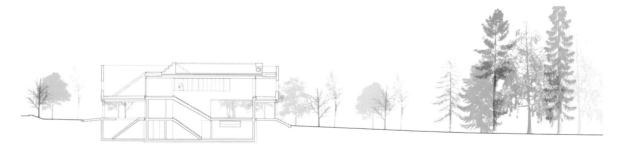

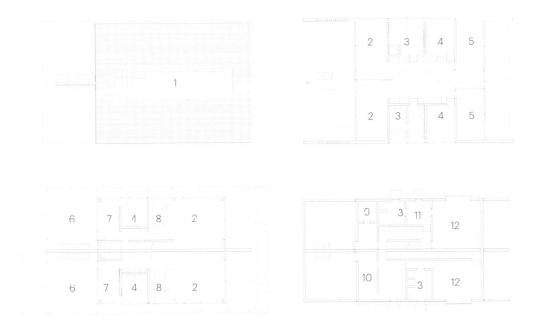

Plans of the rooftop and first floor (top row), and of the ground floor and basement (bottom row). Key:

1  swimming pool
2  living room
3  bathroom
4  workroom
5  bedroom
6  carport
7  entrance
8  kitchen
9  storeroom
10 utility room
11 laundry
12 hobby room

The house has a footprint of 400 sq m, and a central wall bears the weight of the rooftop pool, with slender steel poles to support the cantilever over the carports. The concrete is shuttered on the outside to emphasize its horizontality and conceal the different pours, and is smoothly polished within. The intention was to make the building look like a single large house, and visitors often jump to that conclusion. The two halves have unobtrusive entrances and mirrored plans, with varied facilities in the basement, living spaces on the ground floor opening onto a rear verandah, and sleeping areas on the upper level, looking into an interior courtyard. On his side, Halter built ramps that provide a smooth transition from one level to the next, while installing steps on the other. "I tried to get away from the rectangle, but it didn't work out for me," says Halter. "I wanted a strong form and volume to anchor the site and to free up as much ground as possible for natural plantings that lead the eye to the forest."

Windows are set into the concrete without frames, and the hard Jatobá wood has proved its resilience on the floor of the shower. Halter worked with a lighting engineer to illuminate the facades and the interiors. Roll-down wood shutters can be used to enclose the verandah; they also reflect light, as does the pale oak dining table and other pieces of furniture. Recessed ceiling spots are directed at specific points, as they are in museums, to highlight a reading chair, a bed, or a painting. There's no ambient lighting; it's all specific to each room. A geothermal pump provides heating for the floors and the pool. Concrete stabilizes the temperatures so that the house stays warm in winter and cool in summer.

"Over the past few years, I've learned that a radical house can be very livable, and that has given me the courage to design another. It's not so easy to do a place for yourself, so you should try to express your own character and principles."

Remo Halter

# RAMON BOSCH & ELISABETA CAPDEFERRO

# CASA COLLAGE

# GIRONA, SPAIN

It took a family to reshape a house in the medieval Jewish quarter of this ancient Catalonian city and give it a new life. Elisabeta ("Bet") Capdeferro and her husband, Ramon Bosch, were studying architecture in Barcelona when her parents discovered that the house was for sale. Her father is a master builder, and he decided to buy and remodel it as a home for a younger generation of the family.

The neighborhood was recovering from a long decline, while the house itself was a palimpsest of history from the Middle Ages to the present. In the thirteenth century, it was augmented over the city wall and grew into a multilevel labyrinth of 1,500 sqm built around two courtyards. Key elements were the Gothic staircase, a Renaissance chapel in the lower courtyard, and an exposed fragment of the city wall. Following the Spanish Civil War, it became a tenement with seventeen small units spilling into the courtyards.

"Bet's father took the lead in removing accretions and stabilizing the structure, while respecting the integrity of the historic fabric," explains Bosch. "Any changes had to conform to the city's preservation ordinance, which applies to individual houses and to the whole area. After graduating, we developed plans to transform the complex into a house with seven units for our extended family."

Capdeferro shared her father's respect for the complexity of the structure and the challenge of restoring it. "The house had bones like a skeleton—the main walls—and calcification, which we removed to restore to the courtyards the character of a void," she explains. "In school, you are taught to make clear statements. Here, we had to

Boldly patterned tiles, salvaged from other construction projects, bring color and reflected light into the courtyards.

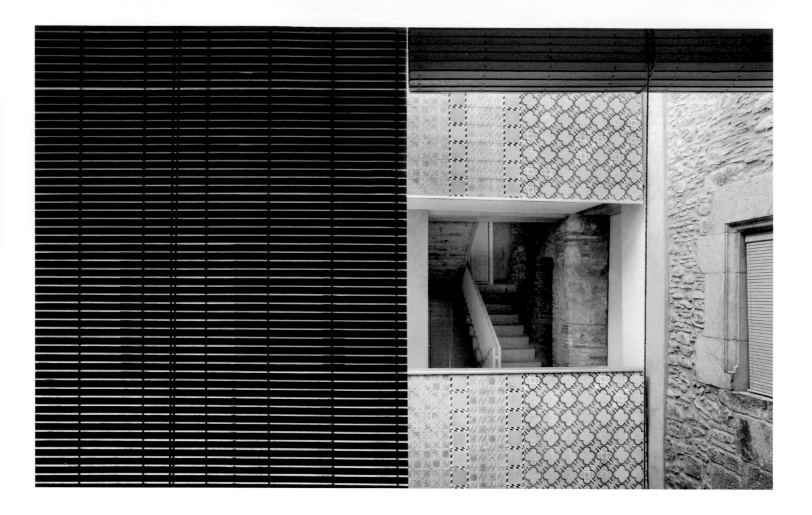

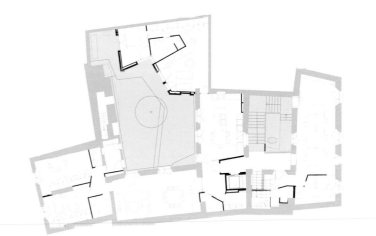

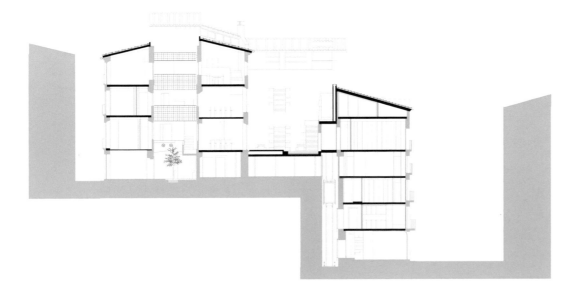

be much more adaptable, and the work extended over sixteen years, alternating between bursts of activity and lulls—when my father had another job or I had a baby—which gave us the chance to reflect on what we were doing. My father had the experience we lacked, and the changing cast of artisans all offered their opinions. We welcomed their input, since they had a deep understanding of the site and how to build."

The complex opens—front and back—onto narrow streets in a dense neighborhood, so it was important for each unit to have the character of a house with its own exterior space, rather than that of an apartment. There are six levels on the side that descends to the river and four on the inner side. That made it important

to plan in section and improve the vertical circulation. Capdeferro's uncle, also an architect, advised on the extension of the Gothic stair, which was essential to the organization. Bosch and Capdeferro designed a new structure to replace a shoddy postwar addition on two sides of the inner courtyard, adding space to their unit and the two above. Its plain, soft-toned stucco and shuttered windows are a neutral foil to the ancient fabric and wrap around an oasis of greenery. Other units overlook this garden, while enjoying access to terraces up to the roof level.

The staircase is to be found in the second courtyard, making the latter a meeting point for neighbors and a place for children to play. The boldly patterned tiles added by the architects are part of the collage that

The architects designed a new structure to replace a shoddy postwar addition on two sides of the inner courtyard, adding space to their unit and the two above (opposite). Their living room (below) is a collage of exposed stone walls and new materials.

gives the house its name. "As a builder, my father never threw things away that might later prove useful," says Capdeferro. "We realized we had lots of wonderful pieces with patina that we could incorporate in the house. Also, the tiles were reflective, and could bring light and life to the courtyard." Later, the architects discovered that each courtyard has its own microclimate. Theirs is more open and is warmed by the sun from the south and west, whereas the other is deeper, narrower, and cooler.

"This was the project where we learned to be architects—like getting our master's degrees," Capdeferro continues. "We will never know who lived here and why they made the decisions they did. We had to be respectful and make our own moves."

For Bosch, it was a continual process of discovery. "The unexpected was happening every day," he recalls. "You would see things and make changes. We got to know the house in different seasons, a bit like establishing a deep relationship with a person."

The project received the 2011 Mies van der Rohe Award for the best work by emerging architects, and the experience of building and raising a family in this time capsule has fed into the couple's later designs. Their own spaces are a miniature of the whole, with polished concrete floors, ancient stone walls, new stucco, and windows that frame the chapel where their children love to play house.

# KULAPAT YANTRASAST

# BAAN NAAM

# VENICE, CALIFORNIA

Memories of growing up in Thailand shaped the house that Kulapat Yantrasast built for himself in the raffish beachfront community of Venice. His grandparents lived in a traditional Thai house: connected pavilions on a platform that is raised above the ground to protect occupants from floods and wildlife. There, they enjoyed cross-ventilation and views of a garden from every room. But such houses are lightweight wood structures, and Yantrasast had spent eight years with Tadao Ando in Japan before moving to the US to start his own practice of wHY Architecture. "I realized that almost every house in Los Angeles has a flimsy wood frame covered up with stucco, brick, or stone," he says. "I wanted a surface that was integral with the structure, and concrete was the material I was most familiar with. Something with a sense of gravitas and materiality."

Once he had found a desirable site— 465 sq m with a teardown bungalow, set back from a busy boulevard—he began to consider what he might build there. Initially, he was apprehensive, for an architect's house is a self-portrait. He approached the problem from a sensory and practical point of view. His top-floor apartment in Santa Monica offered convenience and an ocean view, but it had only one bedroom and the ceilings lacked height. He loves to swim, and wanted a place to put up his parents when they came over from Bangkok. The house needed to be a personal retreat where he could unwind after his travels. "The rolling stone had stopped rolling," he says. "I needed a place I could look forward to living in and I don't like to be confined."

For inspiration, Yantrasast recalled his first experience of Le Corbusier's chapel at Ronchamp in France, John Lautner's Goldstein house in LA, and the sensuous watercolors of Lauretta Vinciarelli. After sketching ten alternative designs, each rising from a plinth, Yantrasast discarded

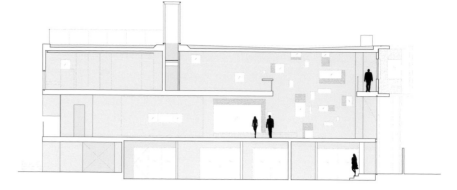

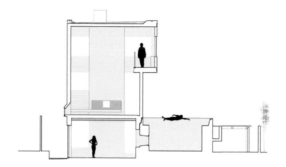

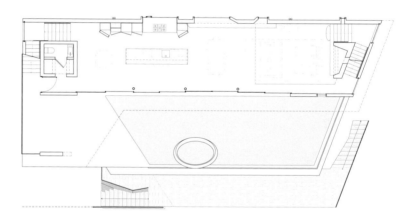

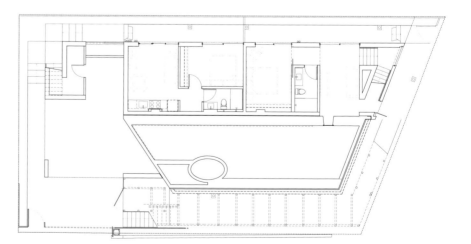

Longitudinal and latitudinal
sections with plans of the
middle and lower floors.

the sculptural options and settled on a simple, skinny block ranged along the eastern edge of the site. Massively constructed of poured concrete, it rises three stories from a walled garden. At the base are two guest apartments and the garage. Steps lead up to a linear living room, which opens through pocketing glass sliders to the pool and its wraparound terrace.

Steel columns support the 15 m span of the opening. There's an unbroken view over roofs and palms to the ocean, seven blocks west. The vistas are even wider from the upper-level workroom and roof terrace, but the master bedroom projects out to look south over the pool.

"Water is a symbol of nature, and when we are in it, it becomes our skin," says Yantrasast, who likens his house to a cave opening onto a river, and gave it the Thai name for "water house." Tiny window

openings with splayed reveals pierce the massive rear wall, complementing the concrete wedge brackets. Light washes down the sides of the free-standing chimney, throwing the board-patterned surface of the concrete into sharp relief.

The upper floor, which gives the open kitchen and dining area an intimate scale, is cut away over the living room. This loft-like volume is animated by the play of light and a mobile of twigs and feathers, which revolves in the steady breeze from the ocean. The staircase leading up to the roof terrace serves as a heat chimney, and the translucent enclosure at the top doubles as a beacon at night.

The influence of Ando is apparent in the elemental quality of the house, in which earth and water, air and fire are woven together. But Yantrasast's use of concrete is inspired by the rich textures of Louis Kahn,

rather than the glossy perfection of Ando's walls. In addition, the feeling is loose and liberating, rather than taut and controlling. Working with his colleagues, Yantrasast designed furniture and lighting to complement modern classics. His contributions include the black-stained bookcase-cabinet that dominates one end of the living room, a folded steel vanity in the master bathroom, and a series of flexible white tables and wall lamps. The long dining table can be adjusted to sitting or standing height.

The house comes into its own when there are lot of people around—jumping in the pool, gathered in the kitchen, or watching a movie in the living room. But it performs equally well for a solo occupant. "Happiness is a Sunday in the house with no one else, sitting there enjoying nature, swimming, and browsing my collection of books," says Yantrasast. "The experience of living there has far exceeded my expectations, and I couldn't bring myself to leave it."

KULAPAT YANTRASAST

# KERRY HILL

# ARMITAGE HILL

# GALLE, SRI LANKA

As an Australian modernist based in Singapore and building in Asia, Kerry Hill has developed an architecture of exactitude and authenticity. His houses and resort hotels are spare without being aggressively minimal; they have a strong sense of place, and put a fresh spin on local materials and methods of building. Those principles guided his transformation of Armitage Hill, a former rubber plantation in the south of Sri Lanka, into a compound of pavilions and stepped courtyards. When he bought the property in 1992, the planter's house of 1820 was falling apart, and only one rubber tree survived. He made some minor improvements and then did a radical remodel, raising the roof by a meter, widening the verandah to shade the house on all sides, and turning a warren of cramped spaces into a lofty living room and two bedroom suites. He also added a detached kitchen and a couple of staff bedrooms, 30 m away.

"Instead of planning all the moves in one stroke," Hill explains, "this small village evolved over a long period of time." It's the tropical equivalent of Jim Olson's waterfront retreat (see page 102), where additions were made before finally cohering as a dialogue between the individual parts and with nature.

It helped that Hill had first come to Sri Lanka as a guest of Geoffrey Bawa, an architect deeply rooted in local traditions, and had bought a plot of land long before he could afford to build there. He responded, as Bawa had, to the natural beauty and cultural diversity of the island, as well as its legacy of buildings by Portuguese, Dutch, and British settlers. During those years, he became adept at creating spaces that respond to the environment in an organic way; he also grew familiar, as he observed in a lecture, with "the ability of a work of architecture

The Black Pavilion (right, opposite, and previous page), a residence for the architect and his wife, is the latest addition to the compound.

Site plan (right) with elevation and section of the Black Pavilion (below). Key:

1   Black Pavilion
2   main house
3   guest wing

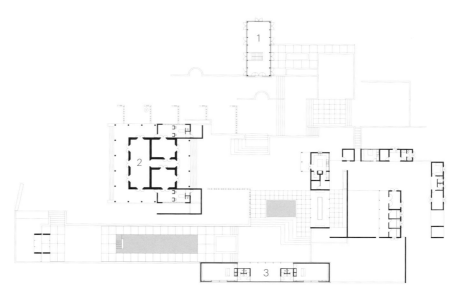

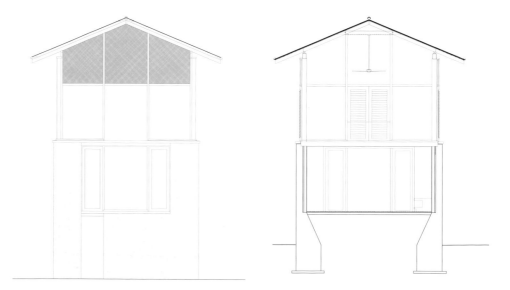

A radical remodel of the 1820 planter's house was the first major improvement, turning a warren of cramped spaces into a lofty living room and two bedroom suites.

to feel comfortable in its own skin, to look forward and backwards with ease."

A decade after the first improvements, Hill relocated the staff accommodations, turning their building into a dining pavilion. He added a guest wing, a pool, and, as a new residence for himself and his wife, the Black Pavilion. This modest structure is half hidden by a sharp drop in the land. The bedroom is at the base of the hill, and was conceived as a cave-like space, its walls clad with ficus. It captures the morning sun but is otherwise enclosed: a tranquil retreat furnished with books and art. Steps lead up to a living room, which opens up on all four sides through

louvered shutters and leads out to the central courtyard. The bedroom is air-conditioned; the living space, like the old house, relies on cross-ventilation. Broad eaves provide shade and shelter from rain, and the lattice in the gables to east and west is lined with glass to protect from monsoon storms. Uninvited house guests have included a monitor lizard a meter and a half long, but the monkeys and squirrels are content to chatter in the tree tops to either side.

"You have to build simply in a location like this," says Hill. "Breeze block walls become load-bearing when laminated and combined with small but hidden cruciform

The interior of the guest house and screened porch. Hill considers the spaces between the buildings to be as important as the buildings themselves.

steel members. Other basic materials include polished cement for the floors, recycled clay roof tiles, timber, and stone.

"The spaces between the buildings are as important as the buildings themselves," Hill continues. "Initially, we sat on the verandah looking at the views, but the additions define an outdoor room. Steps link platforms to accommodate the shifts of level. As in a resort, you don't want to have every meal in the same place, and here there are multiple destinations and perspectives."

The compound is a laboratory in which Hill can test ideas of living in the tropics, as well as a work of art that expresses his

architectural principles. It is also a peaceful oasis, three and a half hours by plane from Singapore. At one point he thought about adding a studio so that he could work there for a week or two, developing a competition entry with a few of his colleagues. Then a client came to stay, and he found he was putting in longer work days than he did in the office. "I'm still planning another addition, but I'll call it a gallery for my collection of Sri Lankan art," he explains. "If I don't call it a studio, it doesn't imply work."

After twenty-five years of incremental interventions, Armitage Hill is still a work in progress. "My wife says it will never be finished," Hill confesses. "I hope she is right."

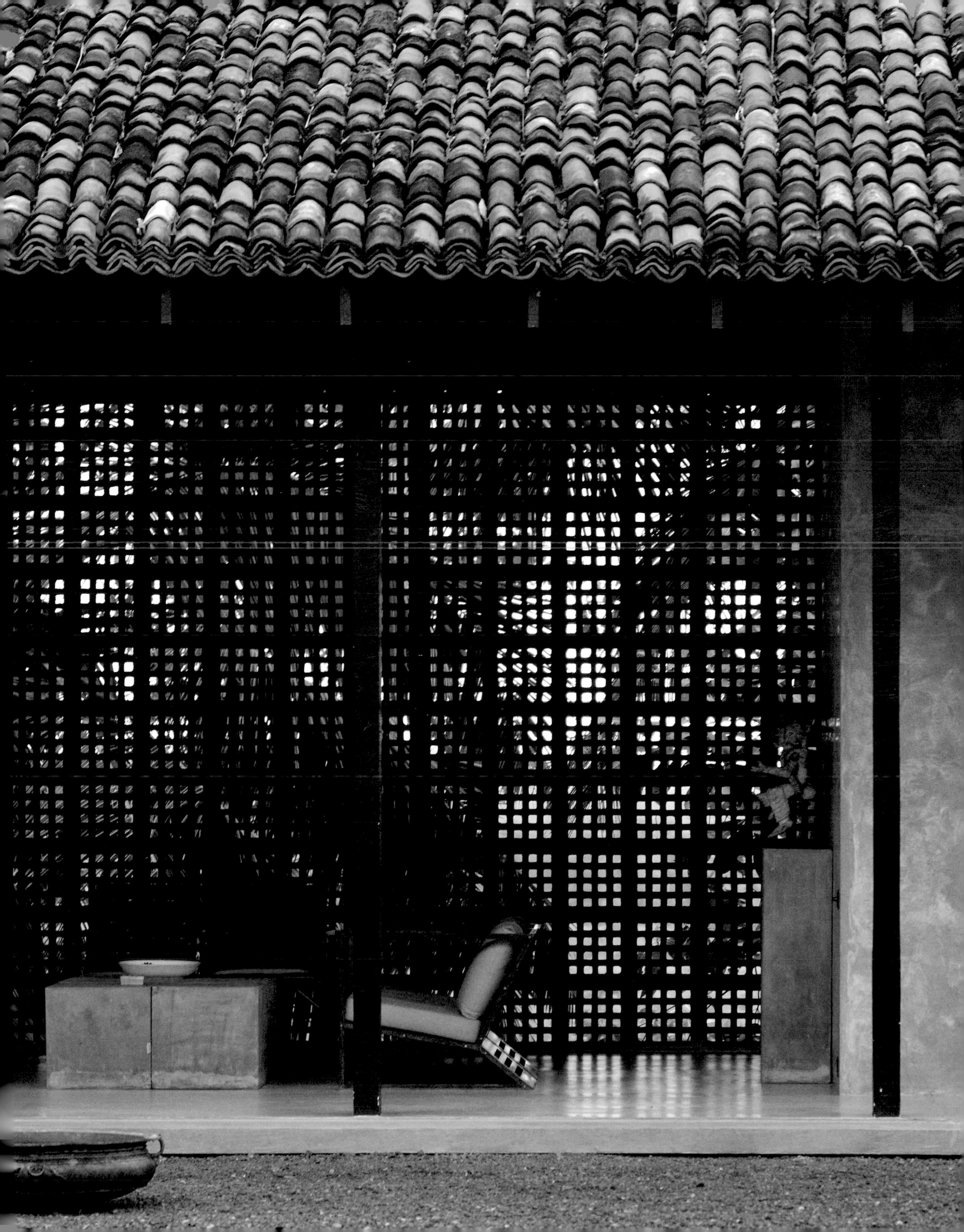

# MAARTEN & JETTY MIN

# DUNE HOUSE

# BERGEN AAN ZEE, THE NETHERLANDS

"The house was an experiment, and it included things we would never have dared to do for a client. It serves as a showcase of our approach, so we don't have to explain who we are any more."

Maarten Min

Bergen, a historic village in North Holland, is a hub of wealth and culture, but it's the sand dunes of Bergen aan Zee that draw the crowds in the summer. The dunes are 5 km wide and scattered with trees and beach cottages. Jetty and Maarten Min, principals of Min2, bought one of these cottages, intending to add a storey, but the neighbors objected and they decided that the old house was too unsound to be worth remodeling. That gave them the opportunity to replace it with a house that was tailored to the environment and their specific needs.

"When I was young, I admired Rudolph Schindler, Charles Moore, and Robert Venturi," says Maarten. "And I'm very fond of Paul Grillo's book *Form, Function, and Design* [1975]. He urges architects to live dangerously while respecting the context, and he illustrates that with a picture of an upturned boat on a beach. That gave me the idea of a house that would lean into the wind and have the rounded form of a dune." He and Jetty were limited to a footprint of 20×8 m and a gutter height of 3 m, but the ridge height was not specified. That allowed them to extend the roof up to 15 m to enclose three high-ceilinged floors.

Jetty is an artist who brings her love of craft to everything the practice does.

She knew the house would be the tallest in the village, and to ensure that it would be a good fit for its surroundings, she made it her responsibility to select the colors and materials. Her chief task was to find cladding materials that would provide good insulation, withstand winter storms and the corrosive effect of salty air, while requiring little maintenance. Although the Netherlands has a long tradition of tile making, Jetty was unable to find a match for the purplish brown of fir trees in winter. She therefore commissioned a rough-surfaced hollow tile, 53×17 cm, from the Danish firm of Petersen Tegl, which has made bricks for Peter Zumthor. The firm was able to match the tone exactly, using British clay, and has since put the award-winning product into production.

The whitewood timber frame was prefabricated in sections to minimize work on-site. The eaves are trimmed with zinc pre-treated against ionization, while the window frames are made of untreated iroko, an FSC-approved African hardwood. To determine the placement of windows in the new house, Jetty climbed onto the roof of the old bungalow and painted the views she wanted to see. That exercise translated into horizontal strips framing the North Sea, which is 300 m away, and a huge window

Inspired by upturned boats on the beach, the architects created a three-level house that hugs the sand dunes. It is clad in custom-designed hollow tiles that match the purple-brown of neighboring tree trunks. Below, plans of the ground and first floors. Key:

1 bathroom
2 entrance
3 storage
4 library
5 studio
6 living area

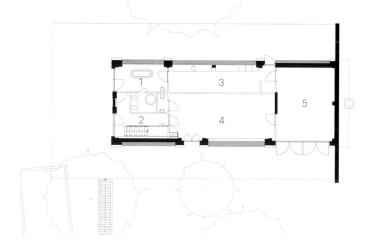

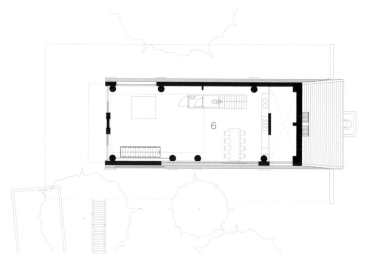

# BRIGITTE SHIM & HOWARD SUTCLIFFE

# HARRISON ISLAND CAMP

# GEORGIAN BAY, CANADA

Summers are a short and precious commodity in Canada, as they are in other northern countries, so the urge to escape the city grows strong as the ice melts. The husband-and-wife partnership of Howard Sutcliffe and Brigitte Shim had built a small house for themselves near their studio in Toronto, as well as completing country houses for clients all over Ontario. In each case, the location was a given, and the architects turned it to best advantage.

"It's quite a challenge to find a site for yourself, searching for the right landscape," says Shim. "We looked at beautiful waterfront sites close to a forest, but found those a bit claustrophobic. Instead, we searched for a rocky landscape with a big horizon line on the Great Lakes, where the weather changes very quickly. Moving clouds, very dynamic—a mystical environment. It's hard to find property

that feels remote. And, although it's nice to know people are around, you don't want to see any of them."

After a lengthy search, the architects found a 4-hectare, south-facing plot on the shore of Harrison Island in Georgian Bay, a large extension of Lake Huron, just over two hours by car from Toronto. The island forms part of the Thirty Thousand Islands, the largest fresh-water archipelago in the world, and one of Canada's sixteen UNESCO-designated biosphere reserves. It is also part of the Canadian shield, a vast expanse of rock 4 billion years old, scraped smooth by glaciers. The regulations allow one to build a main cabin and up to three sleeping cabins on the islands to within 8 m of the water.

Respect for the land, a short building season, and the logistics of transporting

The house was assembled
from structural insulated
panels on a low-tech steel
frame. It is supported on
screw jacks drilled into the
rock to reduce its impact
on the environment.

"Because the house is seasonal, we wanted it to have the open, light character of a tent rather than a barn."

Brigitte Shim

materials in a small boat dictated a prefabricated structure that would sit lightly on the rock. The architects do everything in tandem, so they built lots of models and discussed all the options for their simple program of sitting and eating, with separate places for sleeping and bathing. For the roof, floor, and walls, they designed structural insulated panels—measuring 1.2×2.4m—that could be quickly assembled on a low-tech steel frame. Working closely with the millwork company that fabricated the panels, they ensured

that each could be carried by two people over rough terrain. For lack of local labor, the manufacturer sent a team to the island, to camp out and handle the assembly. The shell was completed in the first summer, the whole project the following year.

The main, 100 sq m cabin is clad in corten steel—one of the architects' favorite materials—which requires no maintenance and blends into the landscape. To eliminate unsightly concrete base walls, the cabin is supported on screw jacks that are drilled

into the rock and will leave almost no trace. Wooden walkways link the cabin to a sleeping pavilion and wash house, offering a barefoot architectural promenade through the trees. This is why the owners call their retreat a camp. "Because the house is seasonal, we wanted it to have the open, light character of a tent rather than a barn," says Shim. "The roof, supported on slender rafters, is cut in two by an industrial skylight, and doors swing open to dematerialize the walls."

Both the skylight and the doors provide light and ventilation, and can be opened or closed in sections to take account of prevailing winds. A projecting canopy shades the large windows on the south side, and these can be screened with sliding plexiglas panels to reduce the glare of sunlight off the water. A narrow horizontal window looks out to the forest on the north side. The cabin's width is determined by the structural panels, so the interior is quite narrow and taut.

Every surface is well insulated, and interior cladding enriches the entire space. Floor and walls are dark-stained larch; the shaped plywood ceiling panels were pre-stained with pine tar and finished on-site. Rift-cut Douglas fir has been used for the joinery, and Sutcliffe has turned the construction-grade plywood end panels into abstract works of art. One features a constellation, of the kind that can be glimpsed on a clear night, while the other was inspired by the driving rain that appears in Japanese prints.

"It's a huge pleasure to come here, as often as we can, from early May to late October," says Shim. "Our place is rocky and tidal, so it discourages people from roaring around in speedboats. Everything is open during the day, and at night, with the insect screen drawn across. You're inside but in a way that makes the outside seem better, framing and articulating different views of the landscape."

An industrial skylight opens
to vent hot air. A projecting
canopy shades windows
on the south side, and sliding
plexiglas panels reduce the
glare of sunlight off the water.

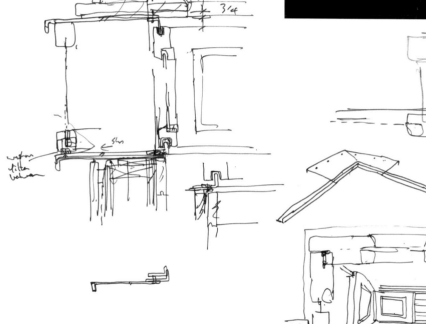

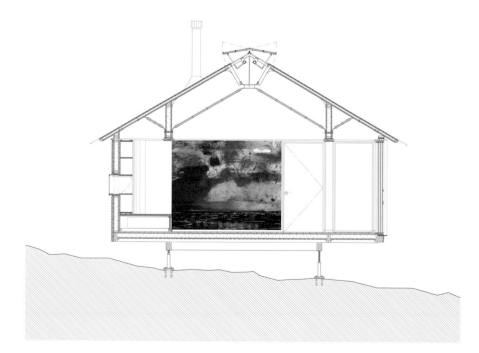

# BENNY GOVAERT

# VILLA ROCES

# BRUGES

"With a client," says Benny Govaert, "you visit the site and discuss what they want; you develop a concept and it's done. Working for yourself, you may have ten ideas in your head and it's really hard to choose just one. In addition, you have a limited budget and are not working to a deadline." Govaert and his wife, Martine Neirinck, found an ideal, 70×30 m site in the green belt of Bruges, 5 km from his office, but waited two years before deciding what to build on it.

"It had to be a horizontal block to play off the verticality of the trees," Govaert explains, "oriented to face the forest and away from neighboring houses. I wanted a repetitive, industrial structure, and that translated into a glass pavilion set against a boundary wall to pull in plenty of natural light but give ourselves privacy. The 54 m long wall is a background, extending from one end of the plot to the other."

Govaert is known for his minimalist houses and apartment buildings, and his heroes include Richard Neutra, Mies van der Rohe, and Kazimir Malevich—for the high tension of his abstract paintings. Govaert also admires the reticence of much Danish architecture: buildings that are good but don't draw attention to themselves. After he and his wife had agreed on the concepts of purity and simplicity, Govaert designed the house as a steel-framed container, a story-and-a-half high, fully glazed on three sides. The module size of 2.7 m was determined by the maximum width of a standard glass panel; anything over that costs twice as much. The taut expanses of glass catch reflections, and panels swing open onto the lawn and a lap pool that is sunk a half-story below ground and inset into one end of the house. What distinguishes this pavilion from Philip Johnson's Glass House (see page 159) is the balance of solidity and transparency, which provides physical and psychological comfort.

One enters either from a narrow path between the boundary wall and the solid

The glass facade faces southwest for maximum exposure to the sun. In summer, it is shaded by trees; in winter, it absorbs the warmth.

Longitudinal section with plans of the basement and ground floor (right, from top). Key:

1 bathroom
2 bedroom
3 living room
4 swimming pool
5 dining room
6 kitchen

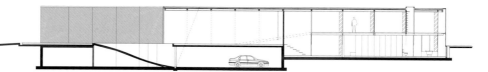

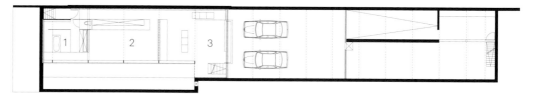

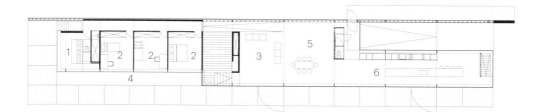

rear wall of the house, both faced with afrormosia boards, or from an underground garage accessed by a ramp. A room-height door and steps from the basement lead into an all-white, light-filled interior. To one side is a linear kitchen and dining counter, which can be closed off from the lofty living area at the center of the house by means of a large sliding door. Mies's Brno chairs sit either side of a folded steel dining table, and these items, too, are white. A blue sectional sofa faces an open hearth. To the rear of the living room a ramp leads up to three children's bedrooms, while cantilevered steel steps descend to a

television room and the master suite, which is on the same level as the pool. Nothing could be simpler, but the shifts of floor level and ceiling heights impart an energy to the well-proportioned spaces that makes the house feel more intimate than its 532 sq m would suggest.

The expanses of white throw every detail into relief, and the kitchen clerestory and window on the ramp assume a greater importance for being the only openings in the rear wall. Mies would applaud the quality of the finishes and detailing, but this is something Govaert strives for

The lap pool casts rippling patterns of light into the sunken master suite. Between the fireplace and the sitting area, steps lead up to the ground level.

in all his buildings. Fortunately, he has found contractors with the level of skill to match his high expectations.

The glass facade faces southwest for maximum exposure to the sun while also being shaded by trees, which cast their shadows through the house and across the walls. In winter, when the branches are bare, the sun warms the house, and only on cloudy days do the owners need to turn on the heating. The pool casts rippling patterns of light into the master bedroom. Roll-down blinds give a reassuring sense of enclosure at night.

"The name of the house includes the initials of my children, and it also happens to be a brand of roller skate," says Govaert. "I've learned a lot from the experience of living here. Every time I return from a trip, I go, 'Wow, it's so beautiful!' We are constantly aware of the changing light and seasons. In summer, my children say it's like being away on holiday. And, as a result of deliberating over the design of my house, I am more sensitive to the needs of my clients and take more time with them before pushing them in a particular direction."

BENNY GOVAERT

# TOD WILLIAMS & BILLIE TSIEN

# WEEKEND HOUSE

# NEW YORK

On fine weekends, New Yorkers feel compelled to flee the city, jamming the parkways and beaches. Tod Williams and Billie Tsien, husband-and-wife founders of the studio that bears their names, have a much smarter strategy: their country retreat is located just a few blocks from their Manhattan apartment, on a rooftop overlooking Central Park. It's a minimal, 82 sq m structure of steel and glass that's as tightly planned as a yacht, but sliders open onto a terrace that wraps around three sides. And the views—of high-rises and Frederick Law Olmsted's landscape to the north—are an ideal fusion of nature and urbanity.

Tall buildings to the south provide shade, while breezes supply cross-ventilation, ensuring that the house stays cool on all but the hottest days. "In winter, we need very little heat," says Williams. "We've had windows open in January, and I've used the outdoor shower in the snow. In a storm, it's like being in a boat, with the wind whistling around us, but without the rocking."

Before Woody Allen started making movies in Europe, he expressed the wish that everything, including the Rocky Mountains, could be found within walking distance of Fifth Avenue. Williams and Tsien share his passion for the city, and loved the view from their top-floor apartment above Carnegie Hall. Under threat of eviction, they asked a realtor to find "something weird that no one wanted," and she showed them an illegal addition atop a 1940s condo block. They took it immediately, and the condo board allowed them to rebuild, provided they stayed within the existing footprint.

The challenge of building something so small took the architects back to the early years of their practice, as well as drawing on their long experience of negotiating permits and solving problems. To reach the terrace, one takes a small elevator to the twenty-second floor and a narrow stair to the roof, so building materials had to be craned in and out. That required the eastbound lanes of Central Park South to be closed on two

Saturday mornings, as trucks carried off the debris of the old structure and brought in the elements from which the shell of the new building would be assembled. To support its weight, a horizontal truss was formed by attaching a steel grid to the masonry at the rear. Two steel columns hold up the front edge of the flat roof plane, and the open living area is enclosed in glass on three sides.

"We've never owned a full-size refrigerator, washer, or drier—so we don't miss those things," says Williams. "We read books on an e-reader, and the view provides the art. Mostly, we sleep in the living room, although we do have a darkened bedroom the size of a broom closet. We use the house on weekends and try to find a day or two during the week to get away from the clutter of daily life. By the time we finally had to leave Carnegie Hall, we had accumulated so many books that we needed another apartment and bought an equivalent space nearby."

Natural materials complement the plantings that frame the terrace. Solid walls to the rear are plastered in a sand finish that reveals the trowel marks. Three kinds of stone were imported from Brazil: basalt, crystalline white marble, and blue-black granite, which was flamed and brushed to pave the terrace. Built-in cabinets are made of shedua, a wood that is used for stringed instruments, and a table, bench, and credenza were crafted from a fallen claro walnut tree.

Glass sliders open onto a granite-paved terrace screened from the neighbors by plantings, and afford a panoramic view of Central Park (opposite and overleaf). In winter, the house provides a snug retreat from storms.

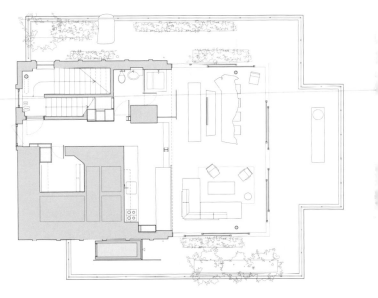

The architects were inspired by a visit to Manitoga, designer Russel Wright's home in Garrison, New York, borrowing his idea of panels that can be flipped to change colors with the seasons. They collaborated with renowned rug maker V'soske on a rug of their own design, and acquired pillows by Dutch designer Claudy Jongstra, prototype resin and cast-glass tables, and, as a memento of Venice, a few of the gold tiles that Carlo Scarpa was fond of using. "In many ways, the house is more about the interior than exterior because of the transparency," says Tsien. "The only thing we kept from the original building is the steel fence, which is much more open than present regulations require. I'm more of an indoor person than Tod, but I feel I'm in the park even when I'm sitting in the tub."

The house demonstrates how little living space a couple really needs, and how rewarding such a compact interior can be. "I refer to it all the time when doing larger projects," says Williams. "I take our colleagues over to show them what we did and to learn from our successes and mistakes."

# GÜNTHER DOMENIG

# STEINHAUS

# STEINDORF AM OSSIACHER SEE, AUSTRIA

Acclaimed as a visionary architect and teacher, Günther Domenig (1934–2012) spent the last thirty years of his life conceiving and realizing a house that would express his feelings about the mountainous landscape of his childhood. The Steinhaus (Stone House), as he called it, is a habitable sculpture on the shore of a lake in Domenig's native Austrian province of Carinthia. Taut planes and ribs of poured concrete are sharply cut away to create a hollow structure threaded through with steps and walkways.

Cantilevered from this angular frame are three steel pods of living and working spaces that open up to views of the lake. A bridge-parapet extends from the house toward a whimsical wooden jetty, the first object to be erected on the site. On the meadow between are located a cubic steel shed, an open dining pavilion, and an asymmetrical pyramid of coke that contains a shower, toilet, and gardening tools, as well as supporting a belvedere. The contrast between this expressive ensemble and the conventional vacation cottages and trailer park to either side is startling.

"This has been an attempt to revive childhood experiences," Domenig explained. "I was raised in this landscape, and I have memories of which I am hardly conscious." Born in the provincial capital of Klagenfurt, the architect grew up with his twin brother in the remote mountain valley

A habitable sculpture on the shore of a lake in the Austrian province of Carinthia. Cantilevered from an angular concrete frame are three steel pods of living and working spaces (opposite).

of Mölltal. He and his brother spent their summers with their grandmother, who, on her death in 1959, bequeathed them her lakeside property. Günther moved to Graz, where he studied and later became one of the most influential teachers and practitioners in the country. All the while, he was dreaming of Carinthia, and began to think about building beside the lake.

"I went back to Mölltal after thirty-five years and hid myself away in a mountain inn," Domenig recalled, "sketching the rocks and absorbing the archetypal architectural elements they contain. I was searching for an idea. The most important part of my work is the attempt to develop out of free sketches a controlled and geometric concept, and to find an order

that retains their complexity." Thus, the fragmented, sharply faceted volumes of the house, which appear to explode into space, are directly related to those of nature. "It is a building that grows from the mountains and rocks, and demonstrates the potential of architecture," Domenig insisted. "There is no mathematical or philosophical theory underlying the design. This is the public expression of personal ideas. By translating these ideas into geometric forms, I enabled other people to work on the project."

At the entrance, broken concrete and tangled tubing appear to have burst violently from a steel-lined trench, as though to reveal the guts of the foundation. This brutalist sculpture plays off the sleek,

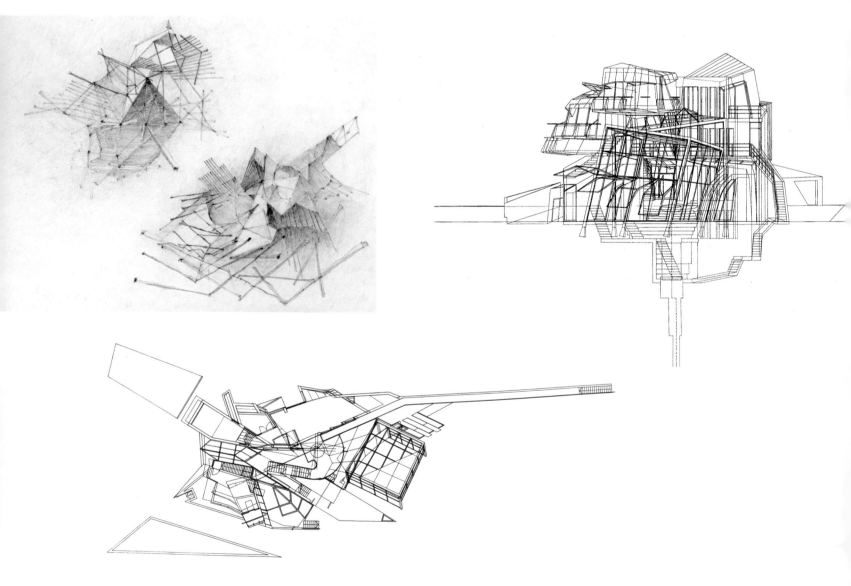

sharp-etched forms of the house, which
can be penetrated through a cleft at
ground level or climbed over. Light glints
off folded steel plates and rakes the
smooth concrete, giving the structure the
appearance of massive origami. On sunny
days, there is a dramatic chiaroscuro of
black and white, solid and void, which gives
way to a shimmering mirage of distant
peaks when the sky clouds over.

The Steinhaus was not intended to be
a prototype or a test bed for the architect's
ideas, but a self-sufficient work of art.
However, Domenig admitted that it may
have inspired his designs for other buildings
in Carinthia, and its angular forms can be
seen in his showroom for the Funder timber
company, a boutique on the main square
of Klagenfurt, and an exhibition building
in the mining town of Huttenberg. Like
an inkblot, the house can suggest many
things, and it is easy to see a bird lurking
in the plan and profile, or to imagine that

the windowless voids of the structure are
a ruin of something that was once whole.

When construction began, Domenig said
that the process was more important to
him than completion. Design and building
would be a personal voyage of discovery.
Whether the house was the source of his
growth as an architect, or only a metaphor
for that process, it is likely to be seen
as his monument. It may also be treasured
as one of the few concrete expressions
of the romantic urge to match nature
that inspired Bruno Taut's treatise
*Alpine Architecture* (1917) and other
visionary yearnings for crystalline
architecture in Germany around 1920.
Domenig left comparisons to others.
"This may be my last work as an artist—and
my best," he told me. "I am an architect
who creates work that will give today's
theorists and tomorrow's preservationists
something to do!"

# FURTHER READING

Dominic Bradbury, with photographs by Richard Powers, *The Iconic House: Architectural Masterworks Since 1900* (Thames & Hudson, 2009)

Kenneth Frampton, *American Masterworks: The Twentieth Century House* (Rizzoli, 1995)

Paul Jacques Grillo, *Form, Function, and Design* (Dover, 1975)

Charles Moore, Gerald Allen, and Donlyn Lyndon, *The Place of Houses* (University of California Press, 2000, first published 1974)

Clifford A. Pearson, ed., *Modern American Houses: Four Decades of Award-Winning Design in "Architectural Record"* (Abrams, 1996)

Matthias Schirren, *Bruno Taut: Alpine Architecture— A Utopia* (Prestel, 2004)

Junichiro Tanizaki, *In Praise of Shadows*, trans. Thomas J. Harper and Edward G. Seidensticker (Leete's Island Books, 1977, first published 1933)

Michael Webb, *Architects House Themselves: Breaking New Ground* (Preservation Press, 1994)

# DIRECTORY

## THE HOUSES

Many of the houses described below may be visited, either at specific times or by appointment. They are maintained by non-profit organizations that welcome donations to cover the costs of maintenance and restoration. The other houses, and all the twenty-first-century exemplars (except for Günther Domenig's Steinhaus), are privately owned. Please respect the privacy of the owners.

MONTICELLO
931 Thomas Jefferson Parkway,
Charlottesville, Virginia
Daily tours by advance reservation: monticello.org
William L. Beiswanger, *Thomas Jefferson's Monticello*
(Thomas Jefferson Foundation, 2002)

SIR JOHN SOANE MUSEUM
13 Lincoln's Inn Fields, London
Free admission daily. Information: soane.org
Tim Knox, with photographs by Derry Moore,
*Sir John Soane's Museum, London* (Merrell, 2009)

MOORE HOUSE
2102 Quarry Road, Austin, Texas
Tours by appointment: charlesmoore.org
Kevin P. Keim, *An Architectural Life:
Memoirs & Memories of Charles W. Moore*
(Little, Brown & Co., 1996)

TALIESIN
Spring Green, Wisconsin
Tours, May–October, by advance
reservation: taliesinpreservation.org
Kathryn Smith, *Frank Lloyd Wright's Taliesin
and Taliesin West* (Abrams, 1997)

SCHINDLER HOUSE-STUDIO/MAK CENTER
835 North Kings Road, West Hollywood, California
Open Wednesday–Sunday. Information: makcenter.org
Elizabeth A. T. Smith *et al., The Architecture of
R. M. Schindler*, exhib. cat. (Abrams, 2001)
Kathryn Smith, *Schindler House* (Abrams, 2001)

MELNIKOV HOUSE
Krivoarbatsky Lane 10, Moscow
Tours organized by Schusev State Museum
of Architecture by advance reservation.
Call +7 495 697 8037. Information: muar.ru
Juhani Pallasmaa with Andrei Gozak,
*The Melnikov House* (Academy Editions, 1996)
S. Frederick Starr, *Melnikov: Solo Architect in
a Mass Society* (Princeton University Press, 1978)

E-1027
Avenue Le Corbusier 16, Roquebrune-Cap-Martin
Tours of Eileen Gray's villa and Le Cabanon
by advance reservation: capmoderne.com/en
Peter Adam, *Eileen Gray, Architect/Designer:
A Biography*, rev. edn. (Abrams, 2000)
Claude Prelorenzo, ed., *Eileen Gray, L'Étoile de Mer,
Le Corbusier: Three Mediterranean Adventures*
(Archibooks + Sautereau Éditeur, 2013)

SAARINEN HOUSE
39221 Woodward Avenue,
Bloomfield Hills, Michigan
Tours by advance reservation:
cranbrookartmuseum.org
Gregory Wittkopp, ed., *Saarinen House
and Garden: A Total Work of Art* (Abrams
in association with Cranbrook Academy
of Art Museum, 1995)

VDL RESEARCH HOUSE
2300 Silver Lake Boulevard, Los Angeles
Tours on Saturday. Information: neutra-vdl.org
Thomas S. Hines, *Richard Neutra and the Search
for Modern Architecture: A Biography and History*
(University of California Press, 1994)
Frederick Koeper, *The Richard and Dion Neutra
VDL Research House I and II* (California State
Polytechnic University, 1985)

GROPIUS HOUSE
68 Baker Bridge Road, Lincoln, Massachusetts
Tours by advance reservation:
historicnewengland.org
Sigfried Giedion, *Walter Gropius* (Dover, 1992,
first published 1954)

CASA BARRAGÁN
Gen Francisco Ramirez 12–14, Mexico City
Tours by advance reservation: casaluisbarragan.org
Raúl Rispa, ed., *Barragán: The Complete Works*
(Princeton Architectural Press, 1996)

GLASS HOUSE
199 Elm Street, New Canaan, Connecticut
Tours by advance reservation, May–November:
theglasshouse.org
David Whitney and Jeffrey Kipnis, eds., *Philip
Johnson: The Glass House* (Pantheon, 1993)

EAMES HOUSE
203 Chautauqua Boulevard, Pacific Palisades
Visits by advance reservation: eamesfoundation.org
James Steele, *Eames House: Charles and Ray Eames*
(Phaidon, 2002)

CASA DE VIDRO
Rua Gen Almério de Moura 200,
Vila Morumbi, São Paulo
Tour information: institutobardi.com.br
Zeuler R. M. de A. Lima, *Lina Bo Bardi* (Yale, 2013)

CASA DAS CANOAS
Estrada da Canoa, Rio de Janeiro
House closed for restoration.
Information: niemeyer.org.br
Styliane Philippou, *Oscar Niemeyer:
Curves of Irreverence* (Yale, 2008)

PROUVÉ HOUSE
Rue Augustin-Hacquard 4–6, Nancy
Tours June–September; no reservations.
Information: mban.nancy.fr
*Jean Prouvé* (Galerie Patrick Séguin
and Sonnabend Gallery, 2007)

FRANZEN HOUSE
Westchester County, New York. Private.
Peter Blake, *The Architecture of Ulrich Franzen:
Selected Works* (Birkhäuser, 1999)

FREY HOUSE II
Palm Springs, California. Tours in February.
Information: modernismweek.com
Joseph Rosa, *Albert Frey, Architect*
(Rizzoli, 1990)

KAPPE HOUSE
Los Angeles. Private.
Michael Webb, *House Design: Ray Kappe*
(Images, 1998)

HOPKINS HOUSE
London. Private.
Colin Davies, *Hopkins: The Work of Michael Hopkins
and Partners* (Phaidon, 1993)

GEHRY HOUSE
Santa Monica, California. Private.
Mildred Friedman, *Frank Gehry: The Houses*
(Rizzoli, 2009)

SILVER HUT
Tokyo. Private.
Andrea Maffei, ed., *Toyo Ito: Works, Projects, Writings*
(Electa Architecture, 2002)

VAN SCHIJNDEL HOUSE
Pieterskerkhof 8, Utrecht. Visits on first Thursday
of month. Information: martvanschijndel.nl
Natascha Drabbe, ed., *Van Schijndel House*
(NDCC Publishers, 2014)

HERTZ HOUSE
Venice, California. Private.
Michael Webb, *The Restorative Home: Ecological
Houses by Architect David Hertz* (ORO Editions, 2015)

TORO CANYON HOUSE
Montecito, California. Private.
Barton Myers Associates, *3 Steel Houses*
(Images, 2005)

700 PALMS
Venice, California. Private.
Steven Ehrlich, *Steven Ehrlich Houses*
(Monacelli, 2011)

STEINHAUS
Ossiacher See, Austria. Tours and workshops,
May–October. Information: steinhaus-domenig.at

# THE ARCHITECTS

NORMAN FOSTER — Foster + Partners is a global studio for architecture, urbanism, and design, rooted in sustainability, which was founded in London in 1967 by Lord Foster. Since then, he and his team of 1,450 architects have established an international practice, working as a single studio that tackles a wide range of projects, particularly those of great complexity and scale. fosterandpartners.com
*Foster + Partners: Catalogue*, introduction by Norman Foster (Prestel, 2008)

BUZZ YUDELL — Since its founding in Santa Monica, California, in 1977, Moore Ruble Yudell Architects & Planners has earned an international reputation for excellence in design based on an unwavering commitment to humanistic principles and innovative design for an extraordinary range of projects and places. mryarchitects.com
*Moore Ruble Yudell: Making Place* (Images, 2006)

SMILJAN RADIĆ opened his practice in Santiago de Chile in 1995, specializing in houses, restaurants, and installations. Larger projects include the VIK Winery and the renovation of the Chilean Museum of Pre Columbian Art in Santiago.
Yoshio Futugawa, *Residential Masterpieces 21: House of the Poem for a Right Angle/Red Stone House* (ADA Edita and Global Architecture, 2016)

RICHARD MURPHY ARCHITECTS is a design-led practice of about twenty people based in Edinburgh's Old Town Its work covers many building types, sizes, and locations. Founded in 1991, the firm has enjoyed remarkable success, winning numerous competions and awards. These include twenty-one from the RIBA, most recently the 2016 House of the Year Award. richardmurphyarchitects.com

JENNIFER BENINGFIELD — Founded in London in 2006 by Jennifer Beningfield, Openstudio is a small architectural practice that collaborates with cultural, commercial, and residential clients to create flexible projects of poetic resonance. Materials, history, and use are woven together to form buildings that are layered with meaning specific to their location. openstudioarchitects.com
David Jenkins, *Openstudio* (Circa Press, 2016)

THOM MAYNE — Morphosis is a collaborative architectural practice negotiating the technological, political, and cultural intersections of architecture, urbanism, and design. Founded in 1972 by Design Director Thom Mayne, the sixty-person firm's work traverses a broad range of typologies, scales, and contexts across the public and private spheres. Morphosis maintains offices in Los Angeles, New York, and Shanghai. morphosis.com
Thom Mayne, *Morphosis* (Equal Books, 2015)

JOHN WARDLE ARCHITECTS is an eighty-person firm that was founded in Melbourne in 1986. It has a reputation for producing exquisitely detailed work across all architectural scales, from small domestic dwellings to university buildings and large commercial offices. johnwardlearchitects.com
John Wardle Architects, *This Building Likes Me* (Thames & Hudson, 2016)

HANS VAN HEESWIJK ARCHITECTS has designed civic, commercial, residential, and infrastructural works since 1985, but the nine-person, Amsterdam-based firm is best known for its public buildings. These include the extension of the Royal Picture Gallery Mauritshuis in The Hague and a new entrance building for the Van Gogh Museum, Amsterdam. heeswijk.nl
Hans Ibelings, ed., *Hans van Heeswijk: Architecture, 1995–2005* (Ernst Wasmuth, 2006)

ANTÓN GARCÍA-ABRIL AND DÉBORA MESA established Ensamble Studio in 2000 as a laboratory that would combine practice, research, and education. The fifteen to twenty people who work in the Madrid and Boston offices take a bold approach to architecture, creating ingenious spaces, structures, programs, and technologies. ensamble.info
"This is a House" (TED Talk on YouTube)

TODD SAUNDERS launched Saunders Architecture in Bergen in 1998, and opened a satellite office in Portland, Oregon, in 2016. The six-person practice has built about twenty-five houses in Norway and Canada, as well as a series of buildings on the island of Fogo, off the coast of Newfoundland. It is currently designing high-end resorts worldwide. saunders.no
Ellie Stathaki and Jonathan Bell, *Todd Saunders: Architecture in Northern Landscapes* (Birkhäuser, 2016)

JIM OLSON—Olson Kundig is a full-service, 160-person design firm, established in Seattle in 1966. Although the practice is rooted in the Pacific Northwest, its work—museums, cultural and civic centers, mixed-use buildings, residences, commercial and hospitality projects—has an international reach. olsonkundig.com
*Jim Olson Houses*, introduction by Michael Webb (Monacelli, 2009)

MAURICIO PEZO AND SOFIA VON ELLRICHSHAUSEN live and work in the southern Chilean city of Concepción and teach regularly at the Illinois Institute of Technology in Chicago. They founded their art and architecture studio, Pezo von Ellrichshausen, in 2002 to design houses and a few larger buildings, one at a time. Their award-winning work has been widely published and exhibited. pezo.cl

HELLE SCHRÖDER cofounded XTH-Berlin with Martin Janekovic in 2000. She and Janekovic now work independently under their own names on a wide range of architectural and interior projects, in addition to exhibition design. xth-berlin.de

PETER AND THOMAS GLUCK head Gluck+, an internationally renowned architecture and construction firm of forty architects and field staff located in New York City since 1972. Its projects include houses, multi-family and mixed-use developments, private campus retreats, schools, university buildings, recreational facilities, and community centers. gluckplus.com
Joseph Giovaninni and Peter L. Gluck, *A Modern Impulse* (Oro Editions, 2008)

ROBERT KONIECZNY established KWK Promes in Katowice, Poland, in 1999. The ten-person office is best known for its single-family houses, but it has also designed public buildings (including the award-winning Center for Dialog in Szczecin), offices, multiple housing, and other projects. kwkpromes.pl

SCOTT JOHNSON—Johnson Fain is an international design practice based in Los Angeles, specializing in architecture, urban design/planning, and interior design. Founded in 1989, the office of more than sixty professionals provides design services across a range of project types. The firm's focus is broad, placing an emphasis on research and interdisciplinary practice. johnsonfain.com
Scott Johnson, *Tectonics of Place: The Architecture of Johnson Fain* (Images, 2010)

DON MURPHY established VMX Architects in Amsterdam in 1995. The twelve-person office tackles a wide variety of jobs, from city planning and infrastructure to social housing and almost everything in between. vmxarchitects.nl

JOSÉ SELGAS AND LUCÍA CANO established SelgasCano in Madrid in 1998. It is a small atelier, and intends to remain that way. The firm's principals have worked on a wide variety of projects, all of which have a strong emphasis on nature and the human dimension. Their interest in colorful, lightweight structures was exemplified in the 2014 Serpentine Pavilion in London. selgascano.com
*El Croquis 171: SelgasCano, 2003–2013* (Idea Books, 2013)

ANDREA PONSI—Studio Ponsi, established in Florence in 2008 by Andrea and Luca Ponsi, aims to connect in a mutually enriching relationship the fields of urban, architectural, interior, and object design. The artisanal nature of the studio's practice gives special attention to design details, as well as to the perceptual and material components of each project. studioponsi.it

UNDURRAGA DEVÉS ARQUITECTOS was founded in 1978 in Santiago de Chile by Cristián Undurraga and Ana Luisa Devés. Currently, Undurraga heads a team of between four and six people, depending on the amount of work. The studio has designed a wide range of projects, from private homes to large-scale urban design. undurragadeves.cl

SUSANNE NOBIS has headed her own office since 2000. Her architecture is inspired by the belief that structural attributes—including site, function, construction, material, and manufacturing process—should be interwoven in an overall composition of space, form, proportion, and content. Am Fichtenhain 9, 82335 Berg, Germany.

REMO HALTER—Thomas Lussi and Remo Halter established their studio in Lucerne in 1998, and worked together on a succession of residential buildings (including the Twin Houses), schools, and public buildings. They split up in 2014, and Remo Halter and his wife, Cristina Casagrande, now head their own small office. haltercasagrande.ch

RAMON BOSCH AND ELISABETA CAPDEFERRO founded their office in Girona in 2003. Since then, they have worked on projects of different scales and typologies, mainly focused on the relationship between mankind and environment. Their varied work has been widely exhibited and has won several major awards. boschcapdeferro.net

KULAPAT YANTRASAST founded wHY Architects in Los Angeles in 2003 as an interdisciplinary design practice dedicated to serving the arts, communities, culture, and the environment. From its offices in LA and New York, the twenty-five-person firm has designed acclaimed museums and galleries, in addition to private houses in the US and Thailand. why-site.com

KERRY HILL started his practice in Singapore in 1979, specializing in upscale houses and resort hotels—the latter most notably for Aman—before broadening his scope to include environmentally sensitive apartment blocks. In 2010, he opened a second office in his native Perth, to design civic and institutional buildings in collaboration with sixty-plus colleagues across the two locations. kerryhillarchitects.com
Geoffrey London, *Kerry Hill: Crafting Modernism* (Thames & Hudson, 2015)

MAARTEN AND JETTY MIN established Min2 in Bergen aan Zee in 1982. The innovative, six-person office has worked in urban planning, landscape architecture, and the design of flexible housing for refugees, starter homes, and social housing. min2.eu

BRIGITTE SHIM AND HOWARD SUTCLIFFE formed their architectural design practice in Toronto in 1994, reflecting their shared interest in and passion for the integration and interrelated scales of architecture, landscape, and furniture and fittings. Shim-Sutcliffe's work straddles public and private commissions for institutional and residential clients. shim-sutcliffe.com

BENNY GOVAERT cofounded Govaert & Vanhoutte Architects in Bruges in 1989. The eighteen-person studio creates houses and apartment buildings of understated elegance and sensitive adaptations of historic structures. Although it works mostly in Belgium, its architecture has won international awards and has been widely published. govaert-vanhoutte.be

TOD WILLIAMS AND BILLIE TSIEN established their New York practice in 1986. The thirty-six-person firm has won acclaim for its museums and educational and arts buildings, which display a rare sensitivity to materials, details, and users' needs. Standout projects include the Barnes Museum in Philadelphia and the Asia Society in Hong Kong. twbta.com
Hadley Arnold, ed., *Work/Life: Tod Williams, Billie Tsien* (Monacelli, 2000)

# PICTURE CREDITS

# INDEX